Sarah Losh
and
Wreay Church

Stephen Matthews

BOOKCASE

The slab of rough stone that lies above the grave of Sarah and Katharine Losh in the Losh Burial Enclosure. It bears the Latin inscription: "In vita divisae, in morte conjunctae." (In life divided, in death united.)

Copyright; S Matthews, 2007.

ISBN 190414721 6

Published by Bookcase

19 Castle Street, Carlisle. CA3 8SY

01228 544560 www.bookscumbria.com

Preface

The Church of St. Mary in Wreay has a special claim to attention.

Unusually, it was the work of one person, Sarah Losh. She took architectural and artistic responsibility for all aspects of the building. She built a church that has a unique presence and is expressive both in its structure and in its ornamentation. The other related structures, the Mausoleum, the Cross, the Burial Enclosure and the Offertory Chapel, are also of great originality and interest.

Very little has been written about Sarah Losh or her work since the church was built in 1842. Dr. Henry Lonsdale, who knew her in her later years, included an adulatory biography in one volume of 'The Worthies of Cumberland' and Canon A. R. Hall devoted a large portion of his concise history of the village of Wreay to Sarah Losh and her work. Both of these scarce texts are printed below.

Apart from these two sympathetic but contrasting accounts Nikolaus Pevsner was very enthusiastic about the church in his necessarily brief description in the Cumberland and Westmorland volume of "The Buildings of England" series, and there have been several articles in magazines and journals.

However, neither the architect nor the work have received the careful and comprehensive appreciation that they merit. This book, unfortunately, is not such a comprehensive treatment, but, it will, I hope, serve as a useful introduction.

It brings together the two key texts, surveys the other published work and provides a brief and complementary introductory account of Sarah Losh and her work based only on readily accessible sources.

The intention is to provide a useful survey in words and photographs that will prove a starting point for a full biography and an extended examination of the work.

I wish to thank Celia Lemmon, Raymond and Esme Whittaker, Brian Lowe, Laurie Kemp, David Weston, Stewart Grant, Gordon Allen, Shawn Williamson and Carlisle Library and Archives for their help.

The anonymous portrait of Sarah Losh that hangs in St. Mary's Church, Wreay.
The sitter has a ring on her wedding finger.

Contents

A Description of the Church

At the heart of a small village a few miles south of Carlisle, half hidden by the surrounding trees and just across the road from the village green, pub and school - secluded, unfrequented and little remarked - is a unique work of art.

St. Mary's Church in Wreay is a work of individual beauty. It is the work of one artist, a woman, Sarah* Losh. In this small building and the structures that lie alongside, a mausoleum, a burial enclosure, a standing cross and a mortuary chapel, she expressed her life and understanding as it had been shaped by love and death. She used the symbolism of Christian and other religions to embody feelings that were intensely personal and deeply moving.

This stone church was built by local craftsmen. It is a simple structure imitated from ancient times, covered with carvings of rare beauty and originality and lit with a delicate light.

Nikolaus Pevsner had to shamefacedly admit the church's supreme quality. He asks himself what is the best architecture in Cumberland and Westmorland during the years of Queen Victoria. His answer is, oddly, both bold and defensive: "The first building to call out, one introduces with hesitation; for it is a crazy building without any doubt, even if it is most impressive and in some ways amazingly forward-pointing building". It is perhaps a crazy judgment from the doyen of European modernism. When he made that statement in 1967 he was well on his way to completing his monumental single-handed survey of "The Buildings of England" - he'd started in 1951 - and yet, having seen the finest buildings in the country, the work of great architects that adorned the greatest of English cities, he could still be excited by this very modest church in a quiet country village built by a female amateur architect.

Sarah Losh was the daughter of a Cumberland squire who had made a second fortune in the industry of Tyneside. With her sister, Katharine, she inherited his vast wealth. She seems to have cultivated a quiet country life. Neither sister married. Sarah seems to have been impressively clever - one admirer compared her to George Eliot - and she was extremely widely and well-read. Her dinner guests

* *"Sarah" is the form on the grave and the one Sarah Losh used on her will and is the form used here. Lonsdale used "Sara" and this has been retained whenever it is the form used in quotations. Similarly "Katharine" is Sarah's usage on the grave but her name appears as "Katherine" and "Catherine" elsewhere. I have used "Katharine", but kept the form used in quotations.*

included some of the greatest men of the day: William Paley whose ideas on creation and the necessity of God as the divine watchmaker were hugely influential; Lord Brougham and others at the heart of radical politics; William Wordsworth, the poet, and many others.

The church is so original it is deemed eccentric or crazy. It is far from that. It is a coherent work of art. It anticipates many of the ideas of John Ruskin and much of the philosophy of the Arts and Crafts movement. And just as those ideas have commanded increasing attention over recent decades, the Church of St. Mary at Wreay merits our careful consideration.

Little has been written about the church. Henry Lonsdale who knew Sarah Losh wrote a short memoir in 1874, and the local vicar, Canon A. R. Hall, repeated much and added something in his village history. Both these scarce sources are reprinted below. This introduction offers a description of the church and an account of Sarah Losh's life that is largely complementary to those accounts by Lonsdale and Hall.

The church gate is set in a wall of large, irregularly-cut, sandstone slabs. The gate-posts project jaggedly upward like the natural rock, in a way opposed to the accustomed formality of a Victorian church entrance. This style of cyclopean walling is also found in the Mausoleum and the burial ground. Further to the left the wall becomes lower and the stones far smaller and the grassy bank of the uneven church grounds, with its trees and shrubs, slopes up to the wall. There are now no graves except for those in the Losh Burial plot retained within its low stone parapet. Beyond this plot stands the uncompromising massy Mausoleum and the elegant stone cross modelled after the ancient Anglo-Saxon cross that is still to be found, severely weathered in a windswept

mountain graveyard by Bewcastle Church near the Scottish Border.

The church stands twenty yards in front of you. The ground falls away around the building and, unusually, the church is at a lower level than the surrounding grounds. A path leads across a short causeway to the door.

The church is built of a yellow sandstone. The chisel marks are evident on the face of the blocks of squared stone. Many houses in the vicinity are built of a similar stone, but those in neighbouring parishes employ a red sandstone. It is likely that most of the stone was quarried locally, and very probably on land owned by the Loshes.

The double wooden doors - one has been replaced in recent years and is far less weathered - are set in a cluster of carved arches. Two of the arches with a regular pattern of indentations or fillets stand either side of a wider arch that bears a series of 25 repeated images of a stylized water-lily. This same stylized flower is repeated on the outer half arch, or dripstone, but this time the thirteen flower heads alternate with a water-lily leaf shape. At the base of each side of the half arch is a large downward pointing cone. All the carvings emerge from the blocks of stone that form the arch and are still remarkably fresh with clean edges.

There are three matching windows above the doorway. Their surrounds echo that of the doorway, but without the dripstone. The middle carved arch around each window is detailed and individualized. The one to the left begins with a parallel sequence of cone, ammonite and cone and then there are a variety of not-readily identifiable

9

fossil forms. The sequence possibly runs from the left: nautilus or ceratites, crinoid or club moss, two flower forms, a staghorn coral and a nudibranch mollusc. The carving on the right hand window echoes that of the left, but here the sequence of cones is interspersed with an owl and bee(?) on the left and a bird (a raven?) and cockchafer on the right. At the top of the arch cone-bearing fir branches meet. The middle arch is symmetrical. Moving upwards from the bottom it bears images of a chrysalis on oak leaves, a poppy, a butterfly, another poppy, a butterfly, a butterfly and, at the apex, some wheat. Each image is very clearly marked and represents a specific plant or creature. Again, in each case, each side of the arch including the carving is formed of a single block of stone.

At both extremities of the west wall is a vertical stone buttress. An arcade of nine small recessed windows set in stepped stone blocks rises from the top of each buttress parallel with the gable line of the roof. The glass in these windows is somewhat obscured by a later protective glass, but such motifs as can be seen clearly suggest the delicate tracery of fossil forms or the brighter colours of flowers in full bloom.

At the apex of the lines of windows, and similarly proportioned, are two stone

niches containing small statues of St. Peter and St. Paul. The statues have worn badly and are largely obscured by the protective metal mesh now in front of them. They are of a different stone and it is probable that they were carvings that Sarah Losh acquired from elsewhere.

Above the conventional belfry is an alert, proud and aspiring, almost Napoleonic, eagle. The present bird is the work of the York sculptor and carver Dick Reid, and this copy replaced the dangerous original in 1997.

In winter, the south wall of the church is often patterned with the branches of the surrounding trees in the morning sunlight. As on the north wall there are four arched stained glass windows recessed in plain stone surrounds. Above each window is a set of

three windows set as a group. These windows are similar in size and colouring to those in the west gable: the central window contains plant or fossil tracery and the two side ones brightly coloured flowers. On the south wall there is a small clear glass window let into the eastern corner to admit light onto the pulpit. This may have been provided as a direct response to Bishop Percy's, apparently only, stricture about the design, that the church was too dark. Again there is a simple vertical buttress at each corner.

The most unusual features are the "gargoyles". These large projecting animal forms are carved out of single blocks of stone let into the fabric of the wall immediately below the eaves. On the south side there are two beasties. The western corner is host to a handsomely scaled, sinuously-turned snake's head. This snake or serpent is possessed of regular rows of triangular teeth and the angle of his mouth and eyes suggest apprehension rather than evil. The snake's partner on the east corner, is a far more amiable creature. This crocodile with his little feet, rhythmic scales and strange skull cap wears a benign smile.

On the north side are even kindlier beasts. The scaled and winged turtle on the east corner with his gently rounded claws seems to be pouncing forward in infinite slow motion. The west corner houses two companionable creatures. A tortoise, displaying all four paws and a soft underbelly, projects precariously out and a snub-nosed dragon gapes upward out of the top of the buttress. He suffered the indignity of serving as a chimney flue for the church's original heating system. The "gargoyles" may be representations derived from fossils which were being discovered in the coalfields of the north-east and elsewhere at the time, but their forms would have been even less identifiable to the uninformed observer.

The east end is an apse. There are thirteen blind window insets, (seven of which are set with small orange lights) and above them is a series of small windows, corresponding in size and shape to the ones elsewhere. Eight of these, in the middle of the semi-circle, are made of alabaster with fossil tracery which can be seen from the outside. The others are of clear glass.

On the south side of the apse, steps lead down to the crypt door. Hall notes that this door, either the door itself or the stone surround, were part of the original church. The condition of both suggests that this is unlikely.

Immediately to the right of the door in the west end is a small well with iron railings made from downwardly pointing arrows. Steps lead down to the bottom and on one wall just below ground level is a badly eroded lion's head.

The main door in the west end is decorated with arrows. The arrows are beautifully cast with delicately feathered flights. They point upwards or inwards towards the altar of the church.

On the inner wooden door frame is an exquisitely carved gourd vine. The plant trails sinuously around the arch, with its runners tailing off in natural arabesques and with the heavy gourds and flatly displayed leaves rhythmically displaced. To the bottom of the right hand side is a butterfly, its markings, body and antennae all beautifully observed. Eating off the same gourd is another butterfly shown in profile. Its wings are drawn with a rare delicacy. At the bottom of the left hand post is a healthy and very sizeable grub.

This wonderful piece of work, done by Sarah Losh's gardener, is largely veiled from view by a makeshift, heavily-curtained porch. To the right, spoiling the lines of the narrow baptistry and cutting across the simple stone balustrade is a small vestry made of panelled wood with its contents curtained from general view. Miss Losh appears not to have considered some of the practical, everyday aspects of her building, but it is a great pity that the lines and proportions of such an harmoniously contrived interior should be spoilt by an alien, if very necessary,

structure.

The body of the church is small, just eleven rows of pews, about a central aisle now covered in a red carpet. The pews are made of oak from Woodside with seats and panels of rich, reddish brown wood from Spanish chestnut trees that were blown down in a gale in Lowther Park. Apart from a small curve at the base of each end, the pews are simply, solidly made, with panelled backs and no decoration. They rest on two low wooden platforms either side of the aisle.

The walls with their Roman cement finish, are painted white, the lower third below the windows incised with diagonal lines and the upper wall marked with horizontal lines with regularly spaced verticals suggesting a stone pattern.

There are four windows on each side with their corresponding groups of three clerestory windows above. Each of the eight windows is made of a central portion composed of an upper and lower blue circle with a brown oval with extended ends in the middle. These forms are set within the framework of three ascending St. Andrew's crosses in a glowing emerald green with bright red circlets enclosing clear diamond shapes at their centres. The leaded segments of glass, other than the patterned parts, are mostly of a clear, but dulled glass, with just the occasional piece of perhaps a pale red or yellow glass set seemingly at random.

The central shape held in a thin black iron frame is surrounded by a four inch border. This border is kaleidoscopic. It is made of small fragments of glass, all coloured or patterned, none more than two or three inches long, with every shape irregular and disposed as though at random. Inset among the brightly coloured fragments in orange, red, mauve, yellow and purple are fragments of imitation medieval glass, probably discards from the

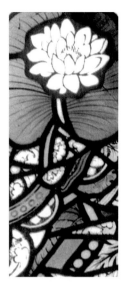

William Wailes workshop in Newcastle. The glass has been restored to life. The glass draws the eye with its small broken images of leaves and acorns and flowers and heraldic devices. In the bottom of one window is the outline of a bearded head. Elsewhere there are fragments of words in decorative Gothic scripts: "MEMO" "ATE". They are almost like Cubist collages. They are the product of a sensibility very different from that prevailing at the time.

When the bright sunlight shines through these windows, the coloured light dances on the walls with a life of its own.

The glass in the clerestory windows appears more intense, the colour more concentrated. The outer windows of each group of three are collages of mostly the imitation medieval glass with a large, vibrantly coloured flower head almost filling the round at the top of the window. The middle window has been blacked out except for a tracery which outlines the form of a plant or fossil. The glass has been coloured or left clear, with, apparently, no attempt to imitate nature's colours. Both Lonsdale and Hall say that the only fragments of medieval glass used form the image of the deadly nightshade to be found in the extreme north-east window. William Septimus Losh had brought back fragments of glass from the ruins of the chapel of the Archbishop's Palace in Sens outside Paris. The palace had been attacked by a mob in 1830.

At the rear of the north wall, at a height of about eight feet, an arrow projects horizontally as though it has been shot into the solid stone with immense force. It is, with its delicate feathering, an exact companion to the arrows in the door. Below it is a small arched niche set as though it might receive the image of a saint. There are three corresponding niches in the other corners, the two at the east end are fitted with clear glass and serve as lights for the pulpit and lectern.

The windows on the west wall are set with their bases at a level with the tops of those in the north and south walls. They are of the same construction and pattern except that there are no St. Andrew's crosses and the central portions are filled with coloured glass. The middle window has a red cross at its centre contrived from two pieces of glass. The one to the right has a smaller ornate gold cross, and the one to the left, which is irregularly formed, has a blue circlet enclosing a white heraldic letter at its centre.

Above these are arcades of small windows that climb the gable. Wherever you stand in the church, you cannot see their images fully as they are obscured by the roof timbers. Their patterning is like that of the clerestory windows, richly coloured flower heads and plant tracery, but because of the obscurity in which they are placed they show even more brightly. The deep recess in which each window lies makes for a changing glow of colour on its side walls.

Otherwise, the walls of the church now bear brass memorials in a way that is totally at odds with Sarah Losh's intentions. She said that the plaster would crack and that memorials would destroy the harmony of the building and that such memorials of death did not belong in a place of worship. The War Memorial on the north wall has a significance in a village community which might override all such strictures.

The roof is supported by six solid trusses reinforced by strengthening corbels built into the wall at each end. A heavy pendant cone is fixed at the centre of each beam.

The focal point and glory of St. Mary's is the chancel apse.

On entering the church you take three strides across the baptistry and stand before the well of the nave, with the pillars of the baptistry wall at either side. At

hand height, one either side, are two magnificently carved alabaster cones. The aisle is marked by these cones at its entrance and the ones in the roof timbers that point downwards onto the way to the chancel.

Today, there is also a red carpet which seems out of keeping with the antiquity of the church's presence. Sarah Losh called for bearskins around the chancel, but made no mention of the aisle.

Standing above the three steps to the aisle and looking towards the apse, in the dim quiet natural light of the church, your eyes are drawn towards the chancel arch, the intricate patterning in depth of the columns that rise from the stone bench that runs round the apse and the pale light on the walls of the arcade of small arched stone windows, each one, as it partakes of the light differently, presenting a different shape. Only three of the thirteen small alabaster windows above the colonnade are visible, and it is only the centre one, with the most elaborate and symmetrical tracery, which can be seen fully.

Beneath these windows glow the reddish lights of three of the seven lamps let into the wall above the bench. These lights - it is simply the natural light shining through coloured glass - are of different intensities. The deepest one is in the centre, above the painted image 'Ecce Agnus Dei'. The white outline of the lamb on a red background in a white circlet, is barely discernible from the baptistry, but as you walk forward the image becomes clearer, but is never more than a shadowy presence.

The white alabaster candlesticks, on the communion table to the front of the apse, one either side of the 'Ecce Agnus Dei', are almost luminous. The

light has been so contrived that, depending on the time of the day a brighter light, which is nevertheless not strong enough to dispel the tranquil shade, shines through the clear glass of the eight clerestory windows on each side. The candlesticks, - they, in fact, have a faint pink colouring - were carved by Sarah Losh herself. They are in the form of a stylised lotus flower. A serrated base supports the outer petals which hold the opening bud and the candle emerges from the flower like a pistil. The lines of the two Pompeian candlesticks are also visible at the back of each lotus candlestick. I would imagine the original intention was that the altar should only be lit by the carefully orchestrated natural light and the bright spots of the four candle flames.

Electric lights have been installed in the bays, and although the decoration is clearly displayed, the original mystery has been lost.

The communion table itself is a slate-green line supported by the dark shapes of the eagles, but the limestone base, engraved with grapes and wheat appears more clearly.

There is a communion rail of polished wood in a conventional Victorian design. This may not have been part of the original church. The base seems utilitarian and is made of a different wood. The rail is out of harmony with the contemplative shade of the apse.

The chancel arch is a beautiful form in itself in a creamy coloured sandstone. There is an inner arch starting at head height with rectangular fillets placed at regular intervals. This inner arch is cut from the stones of the main arch and the

fillets are set differently in each stone. Such finely calculated work implies the hand of an architect designing each detail precisely, preparing plans and giving the workmen measured instructions. Lonsdale suggests that there were no plans. This does not accord with the quality of the construction nor with what we know of the "amateur" architect with her interests in mathematics and science.

At the bases of the inner arch are two heads, a young bearded man on the left and a young woman on the right. Their features are Grecian, handsome and regular. The man's luxurious hair is descibed in rhythmic curls. His expression is serenely contem-

plative. The woman's hair flows back from her forehead and returns around her neck to frame her quietly beautiful face. The heads are reminiscent of those on the Mortuary Chapel and the one of the woman, although not as individualized, has echoes of the image of Katharine in the Mausoleum.

The ceiling of the apse rises from a dark wooden base. The shaped strips of light wood with their darker battens make an attractive geometrical

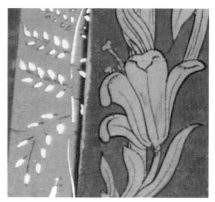

shape. The wooden base is dark and wide and supported by projecting timbers which form a dentil pattern.

Below is the arcade of windows set in a painted wall. This painted wall itself is a thing of beauty. The painting is of the simplest, black lines filled in white against a light ochre background, but all is possessed of the natural languorous rhythm of growth, filling the regular but narrow spaces between the windows and swelling out more luxuriantly along the base. The first four supports on each side bear a rose-shaped flower, seen in profile at the top, almost pushing against the edge of the wall. Below, the tendrils, stems and leaves sway and curve and, at the base, is a fuller decoration of flowers in seed and a denser entwining of leaves. The roses are followed by an alternating sequence of lilies and passion-flowers. The thick leaves of the lilies fill the support and rise to a lush opening flower. The more fragile stems of the passion flowers, the smaller leaves and delicate flowers, dance to a

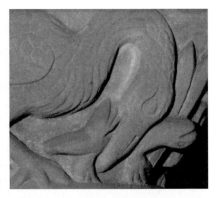

lighter rhythm than the sensual lilies. The painting anticipates the finest of Morris and Co.'s wallpapers.

The windows that this wall encloses are very deep - they take in the depth of the stone seats below and the thickness of the wall behind - and are very narrow with the sides painted white. The eight windows in the middle are filled with panes of cut alabaster. Each one is different. All represent natural forms, ferns or grasses or flowers or leaves and fossils, and are presented in a fluent, abstract manner. A bee visits the flower in the far left window and a large insect floats above the leaves in the window three bays to its right. Sarah Losh states that: "The alabaster is cut to represent different aspects of the fossil flora chiefly found in Northumberland and Durham", and Lonsdale, in a footnote, offers apparently precise identifications: "Among the fossilised ferns may be noted the neuropteris acuminata, Pecopteris heterophylla, Sphenopteris dilata, and Sphenophylium Schlotheimii".

Below the arcade of windows runs a colonnade of thirteen stone seats. The fourteen columns stand on the stone bench and appear over-massive for their purpose. They rise to a square flat pediment which supports a simple stone arch. Below each pediment is a carved capital rising from a circlet of stone. The carving, much of which lacks professional precision, is on three sides only and represents formal symmetrical motifs of flowers and leaves. Two exceptions are the final

pillars abutting the walls on each side. The images here are more unsettling. The capital on the left, on the north side, has an intent bird holding a lizard in its long beak. Lonsdale and Hall identify the bird as an Egyptian Ibis and the victim as a toad or frog. It has also been suggested that it is a pelican with a salamander. On the side of this capital is a curious, crude image of a standing, smiling bat displaying the full breadth of its ribbed wings.

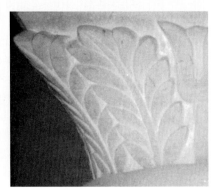

The capital on the extreme right carries the image of a fierce crouching bird with feathers so cut that they appear almost like scales. Behind his right wing, the side of the capital is filled with the scaly twist of a snake.

The wall behind the bench or sedilia is painted a salmon pink. Between each column is a drawing in black, filled in in a lemon yellow, against a red background, bearing the emblem of an apostle. The apostle's name is displayed above, with the Catholic 'S.' rather than the Anglican 'St.' used for the title. The emblems are enclosed by a garland of leaves or rushes tied with a white ribbon in the form of a bow. The emblem is drawn in a simple, quasi-medieval style.

Much of the content, although deriving from the traditional emblems of the saints, is curious. St. Jude - his emblem is a ship - is represented by a single masted ship that bursts out of its surround. Its prow is a large and sinewy dragon's head with a spitting red tongue. St. Simon, normally a fish, is symbolised by two gently entwined sea monsters; St. Bartholomew, who was flayed alive, by a repentant and scaly dragon awaiting a chop from a very large cleaver; St. John, who was offered a poisoned chalice, by a baby dragon straining to escape from a silver chalice. Others are more conventionally supported. St. Peter has two massy crossed keys; St. Andrew two bare branches, his cross; St. James the Greater a sword and a traveller's bag; St. Philip, a basket of loaves; St. James the Less (possibly) a satchel; St. Thomas a sword and a quiver of arrows; St. Matthew, a spear, a money bag and a purse; and St. Matthias, who was beheaded, by a decorated axe. In most cases the emblems are the ones traditionally associated with the saints but these images, even the simplest, convey a sense of fancy, an original imaginative engagement, which makes even the most conventional image fresh.

In the centre bay is the lamb,"Ecce Agnus Dei" (Behold the Lamb of God) painted in white, not lemon yellow, but otherwise similar in style. The circlet is made of half roses drawn in an emblematic manner. The lamb is serious and steadfast, carrying a banner bearing the letters "IHS" (i.e. Jesus), and standing on a gathering of small clouds. It is a strangely, innocent, naive drawing to be at the focal point of any church, especially a Victorian church.

Beneath each emblem is a scrolled plaque carrying the continuous text of the Apostles Creed. Below the image of the lamb is a paschal cross set in ivy leaves.

The whole set of images, so unusual in their character, and so unexpected - their lack of conventional solemnity, their rejection of the standard forms, their innocence, playfulness - seem to be the product of purposed intention. They evoke a very particular sense of the role of the apostles, of Christ, and of the significance of the creed.

Between the sedilia and the communion table are two tall candlesticks, well over six feet tall, made of bronze. A low, curving tripod holds a slightly tapering rod. On the lower half are regularly placed copper-coloured leaves placed vertically on the stem, and above them is a slow spiral of buds emerging from the bronze. The rod supports a saucer which holds a heavy oil lamp. These oil lamps, Lonsdale says, were from Pompeii. In her will Sarah Losh left two gold necklace chains to attach the lamps to the candlesticks. They were of Renaissance work and had been acquired on the continental tour of 1817. One was her own and one had belonged to Katharine.

The communion table is at the centre of the chancel. It is made of a piece of beautifully veined slate-green Italian marble, set in a simple wooden tray. The tray rests on two very fine matching brass eagles, each almost two feet high, facing outwards to the side. They were the gift of Sarah's maternal aunt, Sarah Bonner. They stand on stone blocks which rest on a stone plinth. The front and sides of the plinth are carved with bountiful motifs of grapes and wheat.

The two lotus candle holders on the table are made in a pale pink alabaster and are very solid creations. The base is perhaps an inch thick and is serrated around the edge and marked on the top so as to suggest a pattern of overlapping petals. The fat flower bud rises upwards to splay out at the top into smaller serrations. The work seems the product of precise observation and determined stylized pattern-making. The candle rests in a very deep cup in the top.

During the nineteenth century, and earlier, stone communion tables were strictly illegal in the Anglican Church because of their association with Popery. Even sixty

years later, Whitehead on "Church Law" is unambiguous: the communion table "must be of wood and *easily* moveable". The table is also placed away from the wall and at the centre of the chancel. The priest would stand behind the table, facing the congregation and sharing the communion with them, rather than having his back towards them and acting as their intercessor. This may have been the practice in the early Christian Church, but it was startlingly unusual in the nineteenth century.

Four books - a Bible, a Book of Common Prayer, a Psalter and a Service Book - are now kept in the chancel. They have been bound in wooden boards following the practice of earlier centuries. There is also a small round stool made from a segment of bog-oak.

Three steps down from the stillness of the chancel, the pro-chancel seems alive with creation. Itself three broad steps above the nave, it seems set like a stage. Pushed right into the south-east corner, just below the small side-window, is a

pulpit that can lay claim to being one of the most unusual ones in the established church. It is shiny black, made from the trunk of a bog-oak tree with all the knobbly awkwardness of a tree, four foot high, hollowed out from the back and with a flat top for the preacher to rest his text. There are two wooden cups to hold convenient candles. But the trunk is not so crude: the old bog oak has been crafted to

suggest the monstrosity of primeval nature. Deep grooves run down the trunk broken into four levels and a pattern of small, concentric circles has been made around the trunk in the middle of each stage. The trunk itself is set in what appears like a wave of old wood sweeping around its base - this has partly come adrift at present. Strangest of all is the candlestick that sways upwards to the side. It is a stalk, with five clearly marked growth segments, surmounted by a modest and orderly spread of palm-leaves. At the centre of the leaves is a dark green glass holder and fitting loosely into this is a tapering piece of wood rounded out to hold a candle. The top itself is covered by thin strips of copper cut in the shape of leaves and rivetted to the wood. Commentators have likened the whole structure to calamites, fossil plant-forms from the coal measures.

Next to the pulpit is a stork lectern. The stork stands on the base of a gnarled and twisted tree trunk, about three feet high. The bird's long beak is held triumphantly aloft and its wings are raised as though about to begin the downbeat of flight. It is beautifully carved from a rich chestnut timber. Wings and body are finely feathered and the whole has a natural, alert presence. Hall chooses to call this bird a pelican.

The companion, on the other side of the pro chancel, is an upright eagle with a powerful, hooked beak. Again all is beautifully observed from the scaly talons upwards to the fiery flow of the feathers. Both birds are the work of John Scott of Dalston. They are exceptionally fine but there is no record of any other work by this artist.

Just below the small

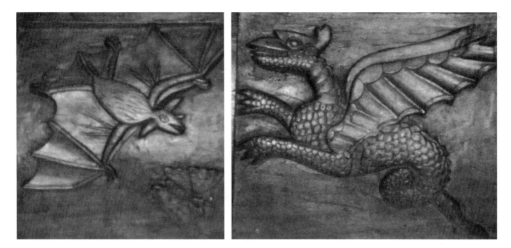

window in the north east corner is a carved shelf, something over a foot square. Its rounded edges are cut crudely, but attached to the support beneath it, and carved in the same style and in the same wood as the eagle and the stork are a companionable owl and cockerel, presented with the freshness of images from Chaucer or fairy tales.

The two most striking figures are the large archangels, almost human-size, that hover to the right and left of the chancel arch. Again they are beautifully wrought, the outstretched wings as finely carved as those of the eagle and stork. The tunic of the one on the left seems of a delicate fabric and follows the contours of the body, her left leg is bent and her body leans slightly forward as though taking a quiet, confident step forward. She bears a palm frond that has simply been attached to the back of her right hand. The archangel on the right has upper and lower garments that hang more heavily. She stands more modestly, thoughtfully, with one arm at her side, holding a flower, probably a lily, and the other arm held over her breast. Both archangels look outwards with their heads inclined slightly to the side. They might have alighted from a Renaissance painting. Pevsner lists "a wooden Annunciation": the angel appearing to Mary traditionally carries a lily and Pevsner may be referring to these figures.

They stand on quarter-round wooden brackets. Playfully carved in relief below the more modest archangel is a leaping dragon, with outspread wings and a spiralling tail. On the rounded panel below the advancing archangel is a bat with outstretched wings pursuing a delicately marked butterfly.

The most unusual furnishing in the pro-chancel area is the row of angels and palm trees that stand on a shelf above the chancel arch. In the subdued natural lighting of the church, they are just dark shadowed presences, and even lit as they

are today, from above, which can never have been Sarah Losh's intention, their detailing and individuality are barely discernible.

The eight palm trees are curiously shaped with thick trunks and a closely rounded head of leaves. They alternate with the seven angels, who are all different. They are presented as though walking in procession, their legs and bodies differently flexed, their arms held differently. The garments, each again different, fall in natural folds, very much as though they were village maidens walking along an Italian road or part of a procession in ancient Athens. Each one is framed by a large pair of folded wings. The angel in the centre has a banner spread across her breast. The two either side stand with hands clasped in fervent prayer, The other four carry palm branches or lilies. Hall says that the angels on the chancel were a gift. They may, nevertheless, like the wooden books which were also a gift, have been made specifically for the church.

In the recess beneath the shelf - there is a thick six-inch board attached to the front - are a series of eight carvings. These cannot be seen in the natural light and appear just as dark stains in the electric light, but each has been as finely and carefully rendered as if it was in the brightest spotlight. On the extreme left is an oak leaf and large acorn. Under the second palm tree is a grasshopper, and then follow a flower, a bunch of grapes, another bunch of grapes (or possibly other berries) differently portrayed, a four-petalled flower, another grasshopper and finally a sunflower.

The only other furnishing from Sarah Losh's time is the font. It is the most remarkable and beautiful work of all and the only one recorded as being, at least partly, the direct work of Sarah's hand. She worked on it with her cousin, William Septimus Losh, who was mainly responsible for the font cover. It has been cut from a solid block of ivory-coloured alabaster, two feet in diameter and ten inches deep. It tapers downwards to a diameter of twenty inches. The bowl has been hollowed out to a depth of eight inches and there is a wide, four inch brim running all round except where two small semi-circular notches have been cut to accommodate the handles for the cover. It contains a shallow metal bowl with small scalloped handles on the inside. The cover consists of a round mirror held

in a crudely made and rivetted metal frame which sits well within the rim of the bowl. The mirror is now badly scratched, but it serves as a surface for five water-lily leaves made from cut alabaster scratched with a branching pattern and two cup-like (lotus?) flowers holding ovoid buds. One of these is now missing. The two notches are fitted with smaller, bud-like flowers.

The sides are most remarkable. There are ten sides each bearing an image cut in deep square relief. The shape they occupy is bordered by Norman zig-zags around the top and a corresponding Greek fluting around the base, such that each panel reaches into two empty triangles at top and bottom.

A dove bearing an olive leaf perches on the apex of one triangle. The plumage is closely observed. Behind the dove, to the right, is a grape vine. A flat vine leaf occupies the upper left-side. Its patterning is irregular, natural and individual - it is a particular leaf, precisely observed with no resort to easy symmetry. Beneath it, tendrils twirl from the vine. To the right is a bunch of grapes. The next panel is filled with a melon or gourd, hanging heavily from its curving stalk, next to its leaf and below a small flower bud with its closed petals. A pomegranate follows filling the panel with leaves and flowers. Everything is seen afresh and then stylized so that each leaf is turned differently.

The next three panels are more stylized and symmetrical. The first is filled

with the rounded segments of a fruit depending from a pair of curling leaves. Hall calls this a pine. It closely resembles the sora, the microscopic sporing structures on the fern. The second has a pair of water lilies, formally presented. With their star-like flowers they rise in parallel from a water-lily leaf whose notch is fitted to the apex of the triangular base. Next to them are two lotus flowers. each with a pair of petals parting to reveal the rising pistil at the centre of the flower. Beneath the flower heads the symmetry is not continued. The flower on the left rises above two smaller flowers and outspreading leaves, whereas its partner surmounts a large flower that curves and turns to its left. A butterfly nudges against the apex of the next triangle, the natural symmetry of its outspread wings beautifully displayed as they reach out from its solid abdomen to fill the panel. Beneath, a leafy plant serves as a foil to the butterfly's pattern. The next panel is yet more profusely filled. Five ears of wheat or barley stretch out into all sectors, their individual parts closely marked and their hairs flowing outwards. Beneath are two small weedy tendrils. The final panel holds a dragonfly, placed diagonally such that its wings stretch out to the corners and its proboscis and tail stretch out in the other directions.

The whole is a masterpiece of observation and design, each panel alive and fresh, yet naturally subservient to the overall patterning . This wonderful creation stands on a plain square stone block which itself rests on a three stepped base. It is positioned right up against the baptistry wall.

In addition, until recently, there were two very fine chairs of bog-oak that had been made to hold two Italian panels, one depicting the nativity, the other the epiphany. These have been stolen.

A medieval holy water bucket from Normandy is now in the Treasury in Carlisle Cathedral. In her will Sarah Losh requests that: "My Verona inkstand to be chained in Wreay Chapel". This is also in the Cathedral Treasury.

Lonsdale refers to "a Jewish lamp in front of one table of the Law" on the wall to the north and a second table south of the door; bear-skins being used as foot-cloths before the altar; an iron stove "cast in the form of a sigillariae" at the west end and an antique stove at the east end. Pevsner refers to the tables of the Law and, in a footnote, says that they have been removed.

Hall mentions an Italian lamp that hangs above the pulpit; "a 'scaldino' or chafing dish, also of Italian design, stands on the bracket near the reading desk, where also are figures of lions."

None of these appear to be in the church today.

On the back wall is an oil portrait said to be of Sarah, which had originally hung in Woodside, a modern family crest and a small plaque to William Hindson who was responsible for much of the stone carving.

The Church of St. Mary in Wreay is a building of striking originality. Nearly every aspect of its structure and design has the mark of a capable and imaginative mind with a clear vision, prepared to select from a rich and diverse cultural knowledge or to invent anew as that vision dictated.

The basic structure of a rectangular box-plan with an apse is similar to early churches found in Italy. Sarah Losh calls the style Lombardic and Pevsner says: "It was intended to be a Roman basilica . . . but much else is Romanesque rather than Early Christian, and French rather than Italian. . . . In short, Miss Losh was quite free in her interpretation, and quite original". He refers to similar designs being re-developed in Germany during the 1820s and 1830s and churches being built in England, in Wilton, Watling Street and Streatham, in the 1840s. In all cases these were built by professional architects aware of earlier German developments. It is unlikely that Sarah Losh was aware of the Rundbogenstil churches in Germany. More importantly, although the structural concept was the same, the imaginative concept was different. Wreay is a small church, built for a small community - there is seating for 150. It is an intimate space. Part of Sarah Losh's structural originality is to have taken the example of the larger early Italian churches and reconceived them to her purposes in this small Cumberland village.

Her approach to construction was equally individual. She almost certainly worked with local tradesmen who had little or no practical knowledge of church building or of any similar large structure. She had the knowledge, contacts and wealth to have employed the best architects and craftsmen in the country, but she chose to train local people and direct them in such a way as to achieve a very particular result. Hall tells the unsubstantiated anecdote of the young William Hindson being sent to Italy to be taught the rudiments of stone carving. In this way she freed herself from the accumulation of standard practice in order to create work that is exceptional in its difference.

The style in which the stone is carved, with clean edges and stylized forms, is very different from the contemporary practice and could be the result of her working methods. Lonsdale reports that she modelled her ideas in clay or drew them on paper and she must then have set the comparatively untutored mason to carve them and not interpret them.

In the same way, Sarah Losh appears to have chosen to abstain largely from the use of industrial products and processes. She was, in name at least, a leading industrialist. A large part of her wealth came from coal, iron and alkali works.

She used mostly local materials - locally quarried stone, oak from her own estate and chestnut brought down in gales and bog-oak found in Scalesceugh peat moss. She had a particular feel for the re-use of old materials and for incorporating the found object within the larger design. The communion table with its marble top and supporting brass eagles, is one example of this, but, so too, is the re-use of the old and rotting pews from the old church to line the roof.

This employment of old materials could inspire innovation. The fragments of original medieval glass or workshop discards prompted the highly original window designs.

It is possible that this re-use of materials and the adoption of the structures of the Early Church had a spiritual significance for her.

The lighting in the church has been contrived to create a particular atmosphere and the chancel has been carefully and dramatically lit.

The church has been conceived with a liturgical awareness that does not side with any of the conflicting ideas of liturgical practice that were being keenly debated at the time. She was reviving the practices of the Early Church.

Most conspicuously of all, the nature and the extent of the imagery throughout the church is part of no tradition. Sarah Losh is recklessly eclectic, promiscuous even, in her use of imagery which is taken liberally from conflicting traditions or seems to be a product of her own fertile imagination.

Some imagery is clear in its use, depiction and symbolism. The grapes and wheat, symbols of the bread and wine of communion, on the plinth of the altar, although innovative in the manner of their carving, belong to a long and transparent tradition. The images of the Lamb of God and the emblems of the apostles are placed at the centre of the church and are central to the Christian faith, but their representation is idiosyncratic and, perhaps, compromises their symbolism. The lotus flowers, cones and (scarab) beetle may be drawn from a pagan source but we do not know what or how they were meant to signify in Wreay. The cone, for instance, is a natural metaphor for rebirth, being an apparently dead object that brings forth life, but it acquired symbolic significances in pagan beliefs as an emblem of the phallus and was metamorphosed by Christianity into an emblem of resurrection. It also has a personal significance for Sarah Losh for, like the arrow, it may remind her of her dead friend, William Thain, and she chose to place it on gravestones and in the lap of the statue of her sister Katharine.

Other aspects of the imagery, such as the gargoyles, are simply bizarre in their execution and the manner in which they draw on an older tradition, but, as is suggested by some, they may be copies of newly-discovered fossils.

If there are precedents for the use of such extensive imagery in church design, there are no precedents for this particular mix and presentation.

The church is not just the work of one person. It is the work of one person who has chosen to work determinedly outside any prevailing practice and tradition. She has selected from her wide knowledge those practices and traditions which meet her requirements with little or no respect for prevailing expectations. In fact, Sarah Losh may have gone so far as to reconceive the nature of architecture and its expressive powers in her own personal terms.

Nevertheless, despite the eclecticism of structure, style and imagery, the work as a whole has a harmony and coherence. It has an artistic unity in conception and detail that very few buildings possess.

However, great as the temptation is, it lends itself to no easy interpretation.

And we are limited in the resources we have to help us read the work more fully, sympathetically and intelligently. Sarah Losh has left us scant information about the building of the church and her intentions and we know little of her life and ideas.

An image of the genteel rustic life to be had at Woodside from Hutchinson's "The History of the County of Cumberland" (1795). Hutchinson was a friend of John Losh and thanked him for his contribution to the history of fossils and geology.

The Life of Sarah Losh

Sarah Losh was born on or about New Year's Day, 1786. There is a record of her baptism at St. Cuthbert's Church in Carlisle on 6th January of that year. She was the daughter of John Losh and Isabella Bonner.

John Losh was thirty years old and had married Isabella Bonner of Callerton Hall, Ponteland, Newcastle, in the previous year. Isabella was twenty. Her family hailed from Portinscale near Keswick and they later, in 1792, changed their name to Warwick as a condition of inheriting estates at Warwick Bridge, near Carlisle.

John Losh was the eldest son, and heir, of another John Losh, the fearless, twenty-stone "Big Black Squire" of Woodside, who relished fighting against the moss-troopers, but was also a very sociable and cultivated man.

The Losh family had been established at Woodside near Wreay since the days of Henry VIII, when, it is said, one branch of the family created a settlement at Inglewoodside which later became Woodside, the family home. The Loshes may have come originally from Newton Arlosh on the Solway Firth, where family history suggests that they were graingers to Holm Cultram Abbey. Certainly, the family retained land in that area.

John Losh was one of eight children. He was educated at the village school and then at Sedbergh, where he came under the influence of John Dawson, the mathematician later known for calculating the precise distance between the earth and the sun. He studied at Trinity College in Cambridge. There, lectures by the remarkable Richard Watson awakened his interests in chemistry. He travelled on the continent and appears to have been possessed of a keen and enquiring mind.

His brother James, seven years his junior, had a similar education. He was an eminent lawyer, and played an active role in politics. He became a Unitarian, (which debarred him from becoming Recorder of Newcastle until 1832) was a staunch radical, a supporter of freedom, education, electoral reform and the abolition of slavery, a friend of Wordsworth and a cultured and urbane man.

Two other brothers, George and William, born in 1766 and 1770, were destined for commerce. George was an enthusiastic chemist. He started in the manufacture of alkalies in Newcastle, but was not a commercial success and went to live in France with his Carlisle wife, nee Frances Wilkinson, and, eventually, five daughters.

William toured widely on the continent in his teens, became a close friend and saved the life of the young Alexander von Humboldt. William retained his friendship with Humboldt over the years of Humboldt's great journeys and discoveries in South America. There must, thus, always have been a strong sense of a personal family connection to one of the great natural scientists and unifying thinkers of the day. William married George's sister in law, Alice Wilkinson, took charge of the family's Walker Alkali Works and other commercial concerns in the North-east of England and proved himself a peculiarly able man of business.

Henry Lonsdale, in his lively account of the family, assesses the four brothers as follows: "As citizens of a constitutional monarchy, they held by the popular cause, and fought as earnestly for civil and religious liberty as the best men of their epoch. They also shone in various departments of English life, being generally in the van of their respective callings. They promoted social reforms, and were not inattentive to intellectual and scholarly culture. Their public efforts were directed to political progress, and the securing of religious freedom untrammelled by creeds and other human credentials. Liberal in all things, and of philanthropic aim, they stood by the intelligent and worthy of every denomination, and were ready to incur responsibilities of no mean kind on behalf of the general interests of the nation".

There was a younger sister, Margaret, whose twin had died at an early age, and two further brothers, one who died when still a boy, falling from a tree when bird-nesting, and another who was killed in a duel when in his twenties.

When John Losh married Isabella Bonner, his father, "the Big Black Squire", left Woodside entirely in the hands of his son and went to live in his Carlisle house. The new occupant became an enthusiastic landowner, intent on improving both his house and his estate. He introduced Italian rye grass to Cumberland, planted copses of larch trees and numerous oaks about the fields of Woodside and Wreay. He was a particularly close friend of Charles Howard of Greystoke Castle and associated with the other leading Whig politicians of the locality, including John Christian Curwen. These men were part of a social elite in Cumberland who formed a close network of similarly-minded people who did much to improve the agricultural, commercial, social and cultural well-being of the county.

Perhaps John Losh's most significant association was with Archibald Cochrane, (1749-1831) the ninth Earl of Dundonald. Dundonald was a keen innovator in chemistry, especially as applied to agriculture. He appears to have befriended John Losh and to have spent sometime in the 1780s undertaking various, sometimes spectacular, experiments at Woodside. At that time a salt spring was discovered at the colliery of Losh's uncle, John Liddell, at Walker on the Tyne. Losh and Dundonald were consulted about the spring and determined to set up a salt manufactory. Dundonald was not a successful business man and probably welcomed the Losh partnership. George and William may also have been involved in the Walker Alkali Works. The works became exclusively John Losh's after Dundonald's retirement.

Thus Sarah was born into a wealthy and cultured family. They had important landed interests, were closely involved with the development of coal-mining and chemicals in the North-east. And the enthusiasms and interests of her father placed the family at the heart of an enlightened, radical, cultured and social network that offered continuing familiarity with current ideas in the arts and the sciences.

Sarah had a brother, John, born in 1787, who died in infancy, and a sister, Katharine Isabella, born in 1788, three years her junior. There was also a brother, Joseph, "whose judgment," Lonsdale tells us, "was not equal to the higher duties of life". In John Losh's will Sarah was made "sole guardian of the person and estate of my poor son Joseph Losh during his life". The will also refers to "my natural son Joseph son of Mary James". He was probably born sometime after Isabella's death.

The principle source of Sarah's biography is Lonsdale's account in "The Worthies of Cumberland", and there is little reference to her childhood or education. Lonsdale mentions only that: "The two sisters Losh had the benefit of a first-class education, at home, in Bath, and in London. Sarah made great progress in Italian and French, Latin and Greek, music and mathematics". She continued her studies in the classics with the Rev. William Gaskin who, despite his learning, appears to have opted for the retirement of the quiet parish at Wreay rather than a more prestigious position. He lived on intimate terms with the family. Lonsdale concludes that she was "educated far beyond the reach of her own sex, and, indeed of most men". There is evidence of Sarah's cultivation and intellect in later anecdotes and in the little of her writing that survives and in her architecture.

James Losh makes some mention of his brother's family in the diary he kept between the years 1796 and his death in 1833. In the published extracts he writes, for the entry on 18th September, 1797, "The children from Woodside, Sara and Catherine, arrived. Tea at the inn."

Just over two years later, in October, 1799, Isabella Losh died. She was 33, and her daughters were fourteen and twelve. James Losh, writing a few days after the death on 12th October, says, "Heard by letter from George of the death of my dear and excellent sister in law, Mrs Losh of Woodside. Perhaps few people ever lived a more innocent life. She was sensible generous and humane in a very uncommon degree. In her I have lost a sincere and tender friend". The choice of adjectives coming from such an active man of the world and his obvious affection is indicative of the kind of mother and wife Isabella must have been.

The care of the two girls and of the household at Woodside fell to Margaret Losh. She was the one girl among the "Big Black Squire's" eight children and remained unmarried. She was 31, eighteen years older than Sarah. If the younger Margaret is anything like the effusive portrait Lonsdale paints of her in her old age, then the girls were very fortunate in being under their aunt's care.

Lonsdale tells of Sarah's adolescent years and her entry into Carlisle society among "the upper ten". It is difficult to extract a realistic idea of the life and personality of the two sisters from the romanticised and idealised writing of Lonsdale. He knew Sarah only in later life and probably did not know Katharine at all. He was writing twenty years after Sarah's death and seventy years after the death of her mother, and in a manner that was adulatory in style. He may have spoken to people who remembered her early years and there is the tantalising possibility that he may have had access to her writings as well as her travel journal.

Some of the information he is possessed of is detailed and precise.

Glimpses from James Losh's diary show other aspects of her life:

"1 April 1802 In the evening Mr. Rogers the poet and Lord Stanhope came in as also did Margaret and Sara. Rogers seemed conceited and feeble minded, but remarkably good humoured. Lord Stanhope seemed an ingenious man with remarkably good judgment". Sarah would have been sixteen at the time. She was obviously welcome at the dining table with prestigious guests.

Both John and James kept houses where guests were welcome, and, in both cases, some of the most able minds of the time were to be found at table.

Lonsdale writes that William Paley "was *en accord* with mine host . . . and never failed as a trencher man." Paley was made Vicar of nearby Dalston in 1776 and six years later became Archdeacon of Carlisle. His sympathetic political views - he was a strenuous advocate of the abolition of slavery - probably made him a welcome guest at Woodside. His book,"The Principles of Moral Philosophy", (1785) was one of the most important theological works of its day and his "View of the Evidences of Christianity" (1795) and "Natural Theology"(1805) were to be influential for the next half century or more. At the centre of these works is the argument for the existence of God from design: "The marks of design are too strong to be got over. Design must have had a designer. That designer must have been a person. That person is GOD". He is remembered today for the analogy of the watchmaker - a man stumbling across a watch in a field, would naturally presume a maker. Paley died in 1805 when Sarah was nineteen, and Paley's visits to Woodside must have been mostly in the 1780s and 1790s, before he was made Vicar of Bishopwearmouth in 1795 and sub-dean of Lincoln Cathedral. Nevertheless, the ideas of one of the most exciting thinkers of his generation must have left their mark.

There were others from the Carlisle area of almost equal eminence. Dean Isaac Milner (1750 - 1820) was an enormous personality, intellectually, physically and vocally. They said when he occupied the pulpit in Carlisle you could walk on the heads of the people. As a boy he earned his bread at a loom but fed his mind with Theocritus. He became head of Queen's College, Cambridge, was Lucasian Professor of Mathematics, was an inveterate experimenter in chemistry and mechanics, vastly corpulent and talked with shrewdness, animation and intrepidity on all subjects.

Lonsdale mentions other eminent men who dined at John Losh's table. Sir Joseph Gilpin, (1745-1833) the youngest of three Gilpin brothers from Scaleby Castle, north of Carlisle, was an army medical officer who gained his knighthood from "arresting the progress of a pestilential fever" in Gibraltar. He had served abroad until he retired to his native city in 1806, where he seems to have become something of a drawing room favourite. Rev. Dr. Carlyle (1758-1804) was another well-travelled friend. He was an orientalist, the Professor of Arabic in Cambridge, and accompanied Lord Elgin when he was appointed ambassador to Constantinople in 1799. Carlyle was resident in Carlisle during the 1790s when he became perpetual curate at St. Cuthbert's Church.

John Leslie (1766-832), like Dundonald, was another Scottish connection. He was a distinguished mathematician, chemist and physicist who came from a humble background and achieved European eminence.

The range of people is remarkable for a provincial backwater so far removed from the metropolis and the university. This must have been a very stimulating milieu for such an able young woman as Sarah.

In the entry for September, 1802, James Losh gives some indication of his active social and professional life: "Left Woodside in the morning and drove through a well cultivated country to the Queen's Head Wigton, where I breakfasted with Messrs Lightfoot, Wordsworth and Harrison. Sir Wilfred Lawson called. George and I drove in my gig to Allonby, and stayed in lodgings with Margaret, Miss Bonner, Sara and Catherine." It is interesting to note how Sarah and Katharine, together with Aunt Margaret and John's sister-in-law, (who lived in Brisco, next to Woodside) seem to have formed a small unit and were holidaying together in what was then a fashionable watering place on the Cumberland coast.

Just before Christmas that year, James casts his critical, worldly eye, over his brother's prosperous estate: "At Woodside. I was much pleased looking at the plantations; everything seems well planned; but not accurately furnished. The wood upon the estate is now of great value."

The two families visited each other from time to time. In August, 1804, James went with his wife Cecilia to Woodside. Cecilia's sister was already staying there, as were Sarah's Uncle George and his wife, Frances. Four days later, on August 6th, James reports: "Ball in the evening. Cecilia, Margaret, Miss Bonner and Sara, who appeared for the first time and was very much admired". This may be the evening that Lonsdale speaks of when Sarah was hailed the belle of the ball.

In January, 1811, James had some concern for his brother's financial affairs; "I am still harrassed by the affairs of Losh Wilson and Bell, but as they are prudent men and have a good business I trust we shall overcome their difficulties. George appears to be doing well and John, though he has temporary pecuniary embarrassments, has a large fortune and great resources". However, James, the lawyer, is still anxious after his brother's visit a month later: "My Brother John left us after breakfast. He made a short temporary will leaving his whole property equally to his daughters. This has relieved me from some anxiety".

On 23 March, 1813, James was in a reflective and nostalgic mood at Woodside: "It is always pleasant for me to wander about this snug and well wooded place and to recollect the haunts and amusements of my childhood. Woodside is now a very comfortable and handsome place and the woods around it handsome and extensive".

A year later, in March, 1814, at the age of 59, John Losh was dead. James's immediate reflections are brief and balanced and contain an element of fraternal criticism. On 28th March, he writes: "About 1/2 past 11 o'clock this night an express arrived announcing the death of my brother John. He was a good and amiable man: he had great talents fine taste much improved by reading and observation. A very handsome person, and pleasing manners. With these advantages and an independent fortune what is there he might not have been. But he was indolent and had suffered habits unfavourable to steady application to grow upon him".

"31 March 1814. I yesterday took a last look at the remains of my Brother. . . . . he was buried near to his late wife in the Chapel yard at 58 years old". The gravestone gives the date of death as 31st March. "1 April 1814 . . . We found a will . . . leaving his whole property to his daughters and making Mr Gaskin and myself Exors".

The will is, in fact, the "temporary will" John had made when staying with his brother in 1811. He wills that:"I give and devise all my Estate and Effects Real and personal to my daughters Sarah Losh and Katharine Isabella Losh in equal moieties as tenants in common and not as joint tenants". There is no indication of how the equal moieties should be determined but the stipulation for the properties being held as "tenants in common" acknowledges the mutual independence of the sisters.

A codicil written on the other side of the will states: "I do constitute and appoint my daughter Sarah Losh sole Guardian of the person and estate of my poor son Joseph Losh during his life my will is that my daughter Sarah shall be at liberty to keep and retain to her own use the house Gardens offices and premises at Woodside together with as much of the states and land there and in the township of Brisco and Wreay as she may desire to keep on this proviso namely that the etc.." The letter sent by Joseph Bewley to William Thain, quoted by Hall, giving news of Wreay reports John Losh's death and then says: "The two Miss Loshes continue at Woodside with little alteration in the family, except that Joseph is come to Mr. Gaskin's with a person appointed to take care of him".

When William and James arrived at Woodside on 29th March, they "found them all tolerably well except Sara who seems quite overwhelmed with sorrow". Sarah was twenty-eight years old.

The following day James sought to console his niece: "March 30th. Had a very affecting interview with my niece Sara, who spoke to me with great candour. She seems to suffer from those doubts and anxieties which are too common to minds of sensibility. It shall be my constant and earnest endeavour to be the comfort and friend of this excellent young woman". It is interesting that James should be so impressed with Sarah. The talk of "great candour" and "doubts" suggests religious questionings. James had become a Unitarian and would be someone accustomed to the serious discussion of religion. And James, who was closely acquainted with many of the great minds of the time, pays Sarah particular credit when he sees her as a "mind of sensibility".

That summer, Sarah, Katharine and Margaret took advantage of the opportunities for continental travel that came with Napoleon's defeat in April, his exile to Elba, and the subsequent Treaty of Paris. On 3rd October, James Losh records: "3 October 1814 My sister Margaret and nieces, Sara and Catherine, arrived at Jesmond - upon a visit of some days, after an excursion to Holland, Brabant and France for about two months. They gave a good account of the civility, cleanliness and good morals of the Dutch and a very bad one of the ferocity, profligacy and filthiness of the French. They say that the people of Holland and Brabant are very hostile to each other and equally averse to an union. The latter wish much to be under the protection of the English. The French they think are still very far from being settled and tranquil and they consider the return of Napoleon to power as by no means improbable". Sarah was probably equal to James's political interrogation. Whether the post-war anti-French prejudice is James's own or that of the ladies or prevailed in the country at the time is not clear.

A few days later James had assembled all 23 surviving descendants of his father together for dinner in Jesmond.

He seems to have stuck to his intention of being Sarah's "comfort and friend". The following August he accompanied Sarah when she went to view the ship in which they had sailed to Holland. Throughout the succeeding years he was a regular visitor at Woodside, obviously attentive to the welfare of his sister and his nieces and taking some responsibility for the management of their affairs.

The Diary offers little further information for the next few years. James stayed at Woodside at those times when his work brought him to the area and there were various social visits. On November 1st, 1816, Sarah and Katharine met James and Celia to visit Naworth Castle and Lanercost Priory. The following day Sarah accompanied James and Celia on a visit to Henry Howard at Corby Castle.

Exciting things were happening in the Walker Ironworks at this time. The works were under the management of Sarah's uncle, William Losh. In addition to inventions and innovations of his own, William had done much to encourage and support his employee, George Stephenson. On 30th September, 1817, the two men took out Patent 4067: "A method or methods of facilitating the conveyance of carriages, and all manner of goods and materials, along railways and tramways, by certain inventions and improvements in the construction of the machine, carriage and carriage wheels, railways and tramways, for that purpose". This was a key step in the process that was to lead to Stephenson's Rocket and the steam railway.

Later that year, 1817, Sarah and Katharine went on a tour of the continent for several months with William Losh. He was an accomplished traveller and must have been a stimulating companion. Lonsdale tells us that they travelled in "France, Germany, Italy, Switzerland, &c." and entries from the journal and other mentions refer to Pont l'Echelle, Chambery, Spoleto, Terracina, Pompeii, Paestum, Ancona and Rome. In discussing St. Mary's in Wreay, Lonsdale says that it bears resemblances to certain Italian churches: in Pavia, Parma and Ancona. It is probable that Sarah Losh suggested these parallels to him, although he was a keen continental cultural traveller as well. Sarah may have seen and been particularly impressed with these churches on this tour.

Lonsdale reprints several short extracts from the travel journal. They are the only pieces of original, informal writing by Sarah Losh that survive and they give some indication of her interests, opinions and personality. Her initial strictures that her intention is to write "my recollections unaltered, not to eke them out with information which other travellers might furnish. Such information I may be glad to meet with, but have no wish to copy nor right to pilfer," promises an openness and an unobstructed personal voice.

Her observation is individual, very independent, detailed, sensitive and sharp. She has a harsh comment on the women with goitres continuing to wear gold necklaces, but she is equally alive to the quality of the accommodation and the delicacies of nature even if they are expressed in Romantic poeticisms like "the dew spread its pearly fretwork on the valley".

Her remarks on religion are interesting. She was pleased and impressed by the "simplicity" of the Rogation Day procession. She does not adopt a critical Protestant stance but appreciates the ceremony for what it is and sees both the underlying (pagan?) object of the ceremony, "to obtain the fructification of the earth" and draws parallels with rural English practices. Even though she feels that, "The grand and gloomy scenery of the Savoy seems well calculated to heighten religious feeling", she is prepared to make a sardonic joke about the severe asceticism of the monks of Chartreuse: "Whether or no such a life might fit one for death, it would have the effect of reconciling one to it". Her comment on "the rational gratifications" offered by the semi-religious community at Spoleto being "insufficient to human enjoyment if devoid of the animation and contest . . . and, above all, the inspiring vanity of schemes and projects," possibly stems from the self-knowledge of someone who, in her retired life, valued schemes and projects.

It seems characteristic of the intensely stocked mind of Sarah Losh that in Terracino, on the Bay of Naples, she could move so rapidly and naturally from the vile food with "the fish swimming in goat's milk" to the moonlit waves recalling Virgil's Aeneas and his voyaging.

She has the self-confidence and independence of spirit to find Michelangelo's Last Judgment "gloomy and horrid", and to see in it a demonstration of the inadequacy of human art.

Pompeii prompted further reflection on the contradictions and complexity of human nature. Moved deeply by the wondrous ruin of the amphitheatre and the intense beauty of its setting, Sarah Losh possesses the acuity to observe that "a refined audience" could turn away "from the soft loveliness of nature" to view the "agonised conflict" in the arena. Melancholy Paestum prompted even deeper reflections. That "casual trophy of human art" made her feel that our "feebler works" will "more speedily decay".

Michelangelo's "Last Judgment" in the Sistine Chapel suggested to her independent mind the inadequacy of human art to "even conceive the things of a future existence" and she seems to prefer Correggio's "bright, beneficent, and blissful" messengers to Michelangelo's gloom and horror which, in another sharp phrase, served "to appal mankind to aspire after heaven".

Her contemplation of Guido Reni's "Aurora" leads to a statement that may well reflect her own artistic aesthetic: "But in his image of this sublime spectacle he has seized on that which creates in the mind analogous sensations; and if not to the eye, at least to the fancy, has conveyed the impression of that beautiful scene which revives all nature, and kindles in the soul fresh life and ecstasy". That aim of kindling in the soul "fresh life and ecstasy" through "analogous sensations" could well have been put into practice in St. Mary's Church in Wreay.

Over succeeding years James Losh and his nieces stayed in touch. In 1818 he came to Woodside just a few days before Christmas. The entry reads: "James (his eldest son) and I reached Woodside at 11 o'clock and found the ladies sitting up for us. A pleasing young lady of the name of Inge was staying there". On Christmas Eve James, Sarah and Katharine, but not Margaret, made a round of calls on friends and relatives: "Dec. 24th. Miss Inge. Catherine and I went to Carlisle and made many calls - Carlyles, Paleys, Dacres, Clarkes, Lodges, Briscoes Anderson, etc." A few weeks later Sarah and Katharine were staying in Jesmond: "Jan 26th. My sister and two nieces left us, the former after a stay of some months. She never had a strong constitution, though she has the appearance of good health. She now looks thin and old and seems willing to retire from the world and sink into the habits of an elderly person".

Margaret was only 48. Three months later the Jesmond Loshes sent all five of their sons by mail coach to stay at Woodside. Sarah and Katharine seemed to be part of a busy social and family life.

The following year, 1819, in May, James stayed in Woodside when his nieces were elsewhere and observed the improvement taking place in the area with approval: "May 27. In the evening I rode my pony out way of Woodside where I stayed all night. My sister is there alone. I rode by way of Blackhall and as the evening was fine had a very pleasant ride, the country being picturesque and in a state of great freshness and beauty. I was much struck with the change since I had seen one part of this road some twenty years ago. What was then bare land covered with ling and heather is now either cultivated or has thriving plantations of larch or Scottish fir". In August, at the Carlisle Assizes he meets "the ladies from Woodside" at the ball.

Sarah and Katharine continued the Losh tradition of entertaining at Woodside. On October 28th James refers to a well attended dinner party: "To Woodside for dinner. The Dean of Carlisle and his wife, Miss Hodson, Mr James, Miss Dand, Miss E. Carlyle, Mr Irwin, and Mr. Gaskin. We had a pleasant cheerful day, the dean being a good humoured, unaffected man, and all the party apparently satisfied with each other". The company is unusual for the number of unattached ladies. Gaskin continues to be an intimate at Woodside.

In March 1822, Sarah and Katharine are "very anxious" over Margaret, who is "anything but well". James was staying a few days to assist with the business affairs of his nieces. On 27th March, he records: "Mar. 27. Breakfasted at the Blue Bell with Mr Norman. I engaged him to act as agent for my nieces at £40 a year. My visit was in connection with the failure of the East Lothian Bank, threatening loss to Sara and Catherine." The East Lothian Bank is now a joke amongst numismatists since it even managed to misspell its own name as "LOTIHAN" on its banknotes. The failure was the consequence of the manager, William Borthwick, stealing £30,000, locking his directors in "well ventilated wine-puncheons" and shipping them out to Dantzig. However, all must have ended well for the Loshes. Along with all the other creditors, they were paid in full.

In April, 1823, Margaret is "much an invalid, but decidedly better". In June,

One of Sarah Losh's gate-posts at Woodside.

Sarah and Katharine went to hear the Assizes.

On 31st August, 1825, James is "looking at the new buildings gardens etc. at Woodside", but makes no further comment.

Sarah and Katharine had been employed in the development of their estate. Woodside was partially demolished in 1936 and remains an ungainly remnant of the building that Sarah had enhanced so handsomely. Nineteenth century photographs present the interior as her nephew and his heir must have lived in it and as it was after James Arlosh had made further improvements. In these years, after her father's death and before Katharine's death in 1835, when she was a very wealthy woman, in her thirties, some of her energies and talents went into adapting the old house, which had been, in part, her father's creation. Woodside was shaped to offer even more spacious and luxurious accommodation. The rooms appear not of their period, but offer an eclectic mix of styles - an Italian courtyard, (modelled after one in Pompeii) Jacobean mouldings, etc.

Sarah totally redesigned the south front. The new mullioned windows met with James's approval. When he was visiting the medieval pele tower of Hutton John he deplored the owner's tasteless modernization and remarked: "Some part of the ancient windows etc. remain and resemble very much what my niece Sara has effected with so much taste and pains at Woodside". The words "taste and "pains" suggest a sincere respect for her architectural abilities with no hint of an allowance for her sex.

The work was done in conjunction with Katharine. One day, July 31st, 1828, according to James's diary, while he was taking tea with his brother: "Sara and Catherine arrived very unexpectedly from Woodside. Their object seems to be to consult their Uncle William as to the best mode of warming their house". The moment is one of impulsive enthusiasm.

The two sisters worked together in planning the house and laying out the grounds with a rich array of plants. The work must have begun soon after Sarah and Katharine returned from the continent. They submitted an application to divert a public footpath away from the house in 1817.

James Losh is impressed with the sisters. On September, 30th, 1825, he offers

Woodside as it appeared in 1880s after a further re-modelling of the exterior and as it is today (next page).

a considered impression of their life-style and of Sarah's abilities: "I passed some days upon this occasion in Cumberland, and was, of course, a good deal at Woodside. It always gives me pleasure, though some times of a melancholy kind, to visit my native place. My relations there are good and amiable women, but lead a life of too much retirement. Sara has great qualities of mind but an over delicacy of feeling has prevented her from taking that rank in society to which she is in all respects qualified". Does James refer to a melancholy that arises from Woodside and the memories it retains or does it arise from his too much retired nieces? What, exactly, is Sarah's "over delicacy of feeling"?

Life can't have been that retired. Sarah and Katharine were closely involved in their local community and had a wide circle of friends of similar social standing. In the immediate vicinity were a number of distinguished houses including Newbiggin Hall; The Oaks; Thackwood Hall, the home of the Blamires - Lonsdale wrote another of his adulatory memoirs about Jane Blamire whom he identifies as an intimate friend of Sarah's. Her prime virtues seem to have been a robust physique, charitable works and assiduous political canvassing.

In 1828, on August 23rd, James attended a "Meeting of the Carlisle Railroad Committee. My brother George arrived. He has not been in England for eight years. He and his family were residents in Paris and has now only come to bring

his daughter Alicia to pass some time among her friends". Friends, in this case probably means family. George was returning home after burying his Carlisle-born wife in Paris earlier in the year. James had "dinner and tea at Woodside; a large party, Sir Francis Vane and Miss Vane, Sir R. E. Irving and his two sons, Sir H. and Lady Ross, George and Mr. Gaskin. Brougham dined with us also and was in excellent spirits".

A month later, James is inspecting the new schoolhouse, the Dame's Infants' School that the sisters had built: "I drove up to Wreay to look at the new school house built by Sarah and Katharine. It is built with great taste and is well calculated for the purpose both in appearance and reality."

Two years later, the sisters were building another schoolhouse: "The old School-house having become ruinous, my sister and I erected a new one, which was completed in 1830. The tything men had made over to us the old one that we might employ the materials in the work. We left the walls standing to serve for a court, and made use of the other materials on the spot". This is the first indication of what became an abiding concern to re-use the old materials. At the same time they built a cottage for the schoolmaster in the style of a house that they had seen in Pompeii on their continental tour thirteen years earlier.

It was about this time that Sarah wrote a series of scathing letters to the

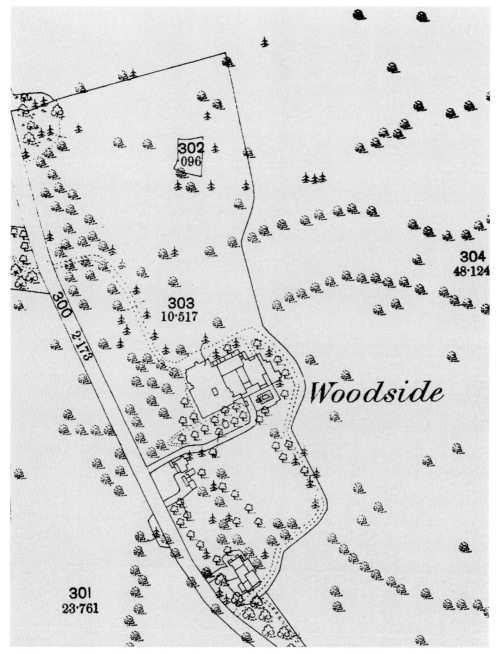

The grounds at Woodside as shown on the first edition of the 25 inch Ordnance Survey map from 1860. The map gives some impression of the scale and range of work that Sarah and Katharine must have done thirty or more years before. In later years James Arlosh remodelled the grounds.

Two views of interiors at Woodside as they were, perhaps, forty years after Sarah's death.

A drawing of the Schoolhouse, July 1836. The chimney is still there today. (below)

Charity Commissioners. They had suggested that there was some irregularity in the funds which provided the income for the schoolmaster, which were administered by John Losh and later by Sarah. The Commissioners are taken severely to task for not having done their work properly. Sarah suggests practical ways of redressing the anomaly. The sharpness of these formal letters, one written on a Sunday evening, suggest something of the no-nonsense sort of character that Sarah possessed. One interesting point that emerges is that some key documents

were in James Losh's possession. He still had a practical involvement in their affairs.

A year later, James is reporting yet another illustrious evening with Sarah and Katharine: "1831 Aug. 7. My old friend, Wordsworth the poet, dined with us at Woodside. He is now an old and somewhat infirm old man, (Wordsworth was, in fact, 51 at the time and James was seven years his senior.) but retains all his activity and energy of mind., and has got quit of much of his pompous and

49

declamatory manner of conversation. I avoided politics and all subjects likely to cause irritation on either side, and we passed a pleasant and tranquil evening".

James died two years later on 23rd September, 1833, at Greta Bridge, and was buried ten days later, at Gosforth, a few miles from his Jesmond home.

We know very little of Sarah's intellectual life at this time. Lonsdale suggests she was reading Scott and Lytton and, at a later date, Dickens and Thackeray, and that she read widely in classics, history and to a lesser extent in the sciences. Her library has not survived, but when James Arlosh died in 1904, Woodside was left to Manchester Unitarian College in Oxford and the college librarian selected 200 books. These included several volumes of Harriet Martineau's works, campaigning for social improvement, ("The Working Man's Companion", and "Poor Laws and Paupers") published in the early 1830's, and Cobbett's "Cottage Economy". But there was also the seventeen volume set of Lord Byron's "Life and Works", issued in 1832-33, and a copy of the witty set of parodies that Horace and James Smith had entitled "Rejected Addresses". Perhaps of most relevance to the church was a five volume set of Pliny's Natural History that had been printed in Leipzig in 1833.

Katharine died in 1835, a few days after her forty-seventh birthday, and was buried at Wreay, on 26th February. We know very little about her. She was Sarah's companion and partner in projects throughout the years. She never married. All we have is a statement by Henry Lonsdale, who, almost certainly, had never met her: "I call them loving sisters, but words will never convey their deep and affectionate attachment. They were ever together in unison of thought, in action and purpose; yet they were of a different temperament: Sara was quiet, humorous, and intellectual; Katharine was hearty and vivacious, and radiant as sunshine itself". James Losh makes no comments about her as he does about Sarah, but simply indicates her presence from time to time.

Lonsdale suggests how deeply Sarah felt the loss: "Katharine Isabella Losh died in February 1835, to the almost inconsolable grief of her sister, who to the end of her days brooded over this sad bereavement".

Sarah expresses her sorrow seven years later on her copy of the Bewcastle Cross with the words: "Two daughters purposed that this stone should be set up; one performed it, greatly sorrowing".

Ten years after Katharine's death she built that most private of shrines, the Mausoleum. Inside the indomitable rough exterior, lit by a shaft of light, is the white marble statue of a pensive Katharine carved as Sarah remembered her in Naples, in 1817. Sarah's inscription, is as heartfelt and intimate as ever: "Katharine Isabella, sweet sister, loving and pious, thou wilt ever be most dear to me; dear is thy pale image now".

When she died, Sarah was buried under the same grave slab as her sister, which bore the inscription she had determined: "In vitae divisae, in morte conjunctae": "Parted in life; in death united".

There is very little known about how Katharine's death affected Sarah's everyday life. Her cousin, Alicia Margaret Losh, came to live at Woodside at around this time. Alicia Losh was George's daughter and had been brought up in Paris. The family had returned from there after their mother's death in 1828. Alicia's later involvement with Penkill Castle in Ayrshire and her friendship with Dante Gabriel Rossetti suggest that she shared Sarah Losh's intellectual and cultural pursuits. Alicia later went to live at Ravenside, a house on the Losh estate about half a mile away, which Sarah bequeathed to her.

Lonsdale mentions Sarah living in a barely furnished apartment: "polished boards, a deal table for her book and needle-work, a basket of cloven wood for the fire-dogs (andiron), and upon the plastered walls a few engravings". But he also says that "elegance ruled the reception-rooms of Woodside" and we can assume that the elegant social life with relatives and various cultivated and distinguished people continued as before. Despite the suggestion of the simple private rooms Sarah did not become a recluse. Her building work and the direct "hands-on" manner of her engagement and her contributions in support of local schools and churches suggest someone who was closely involved in the local community.

Sarah did complete a project that she had conceived jointly with Katharine. The Cross in the churchyard bears an inscription in Latin on its base which translates as: "Two daughters purposed that this stone should be set up: one performed it, greatly sorrowing". On the east side is an inscription, again in Latin, which reveals the daughters's intention: "May this sign of consolation cast its shadow on the grave of John Losh and his wife Isabella. Souls, well beloved, may you walk safe through the midst of the shadow of death. Farewell till the times of refreshing from the presence of the Lord".

On the Cross itself, in the place of the runic inscriptions, Sarah had inscribed, again in Latin, two texts taken from the Psalms: "Jehovah is my light and my salvation", and "Be merciful unto me, O God, be merciful unto me; for my soul trusteth in Thee: and under the shadow of Thy wings shall be my refuge". These texts are some of the few direct verbal expressions of religious view that we have from Sarah Losh. Their choice implies a personal belief in salvation and a strong sense of religious consolation. The texts also reveal, incidentally, a concern with light and shadow as part of her visual realization of religion

The Cross was erected at least twenty years after her father's death and forty years after her mother's. The touching sentiment, restrained but personal, and the concept of the shadow of the Cross falling on the graves of her parents reveal Sarah Losh as a person possessed by grief. However, the manner of assuaging her sorrow reflects another aspect of her personality. She sought consolation in one of the country's oldest expressions of faith and the wonder of life. Weathered as it is, the Bewcastle Cross, which she copied, exhibits a wondrous display of the vitality of life. An unscrolling vine mounting up one side harbours birds and small animals feeding from its leaves and flowers. Other sides show blossoming flowers inter leaved with Celtic knotwork and the fourth side carries images of John the Baptist with a lamb, Christ and a man with a trained hawk.

The Wreay Cross is not a tame replication but a variation on the Bewcastle Cross. The Bewcastle Cross was probably carved in the late seventh century by a craftsman from the middle east. He has fashioned a sophisticated work remarkable for its day. Figures are well modelled and the design, especially the vine that spirals up the east face containing birds and beasts, is accomplished with a fine sense of variation. The Bewcastle cross, even though it stands in an isolated mountain churchyard open to the winds from the west, has weathered extremely well for its age, but it is inevitably much decayed. Henry Howard of Corby Castle, close friend of John Losh and his family, had made accurate drawings of the cross and had published his findings in "Archaeologia" in 1802.

The Cross at Wreay follows the Bewcastle design, but it may have been carved after these drawings or other drawings rather than from direct observation. The west side, for example, shows, from the bottom, figures of a man with a hawk, Christ with his feet resting on two animal heads, and the figure of a bearded John the Baptist carrying the Lamb of God in his left hand and pointing towards it with his right. On the Wreay Cross the hawker's head is strongly defined in profile, his garments flow in sweeping curves over his slightly raised right hand, and he stands with his feet firmly on the ground. The bird's beak is towards the man's chest and its clearly-defined claws grip his hand. On the Bewcastle Cross this figure is considerably eroded but a plumper, forward-facing bird rests on the back of his hand. A contemporary drawing of the cross in Lysons's Account of Cumberland shows the bird in profile and offers some suggestion for the flow of the robes. The two animal heads have disappeared in the Wreay Cross, - they are shown as lumps of rock by Lysons - and Christ stands firmly on the ground. The heavy fall of his garments in Bewcastle and in Lysons's drawing is replaced by flowing robes and Christ's right hand is raised with palm forward in blessing. The top figure in Wreay is not the Evangelist but the profile of the Virgin holding the Christ child to her. Again, the image has been rendered with a strong sense of rhythm in the garments.

This face of the Cross has been treated with far greater freedom from the

The Cross viewed from the south-west.

53

The Cross: From far left: north face;
west face; south face; east face.

55

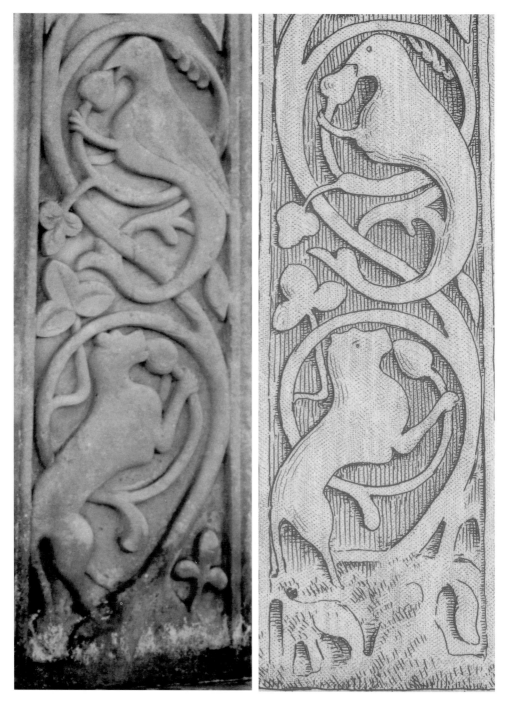

The creatures on the east face. The Wreay Cross and Lysons's engraving.

The man with the hawk. The Wreay Cross and Lysons's engraving.

original than the other three faces. The carving is not as deep, the folds of the dress fall more naturally, the anatomical proportions of the figures are not correct, and the heads being too large for the bodies and the hands. The simple lettering does not have the precise regularity of a professional hand. It is not beyond possibility that this face may have been carved by Sarah Losh herself, whilst the other faces are the work of an accomplished master craftsman. We know that Sarah Losh carved the alabaster font, work requiring a very high level of skill. She must have worked on other pieces. She was a very practical woman who was closely involved with the details of her work and would want to appreciate the technical aspects. On the other hand, even though she was very self-effacing, we might reasonably expect there to be a record of her having done such work

The superbly unified design of the east side best shows the process by which the Bewcastle Cross has been reinvented. The curving stem of the vine is imitated in Wreay, but, following the drawing, it is narrower and more elegant. The robust animals and birds on the original are rendered flatly in the drawing but are revivified in the Wreay Cross, bodies seem weighted naturally and there is a sense of observed movement.

In Bewcastle the top of the cross has been lost. The Wreay obelisk bears a well turned Celtic cross.

The Bewcastle Cross has been re-invented in Wreay. The old cross with its weathered surface and its suggestions of shape and form has prompted a carving that is clean and fresh and delights in the flow of line and form and the stylized suggestion of animation in bird and beast.

It is difficult to give a date for the erection of the Cross. The inscription about the one sister who erected it "greatly sorrowing" implies that it was erected in the years immediately following Katharine's death. However, Sarah makes no mention of it in the memorandum she wrote about the church (see below). Her discussion of the burial ground in this document mentions an additional area of land that was walled round to replace the area that was lost nearer the church. This area corresponds with the site of the Cross. A map, drawn by Sarah Losh from an indenture with the Dean and Chapter and dated 1843, marks the enclosing walls very clearly, and does not indicate the existence of the Cross. If the map is correct and comprehensive, then the Cross cannot have been erected before 1843. To complicate matters further, Hall says that the Cross is beyond the graveyard extension.

In 1835, the ancient church of St. Perran, or St. Piran, at Perranzabuloe was uncovered by the shifting sands on the coast of Cornwall. A letter written to the Editor of the "West Briton" on September 15th, 1835, by William Michell, imparts

A detail from the frontispiece to "Peranzabuloe, the Lost Church Found" by C. Trelawney Collins (1836), showing the sort of rudimentary image from which Sarah Losh might have made her "exact copy".

some of the excitement of the discovery:

"Sir,

I have just removed the sand from the oldest church in this parish, which appears to have been overwhelmed by it, according to tradition, supported faintly by records, 500 or 600 years ago. This church is probably one of the most ancient ever laid open, and wants nothing to render it as complete as when first erected except its rood and doors. The length of the church within the walls is 25 feet; without, 30; the breadth within, 12$\frac{1}{2}$ feet; and the height of the walls the same. At the eastern end is a neat altar of stone, covered with lime, 4 feet long, by 2$\frac{1}{2}$ wide, and 3 feet high. Eight inches above the centre of the altar is a recess in the wall, in which probably stood a crucifix, and on the north side of the altar is a small doorway through which the priest must have entered. The chancel was exactly 6 feet, leaving 19 for the congregation, who were accommodated with stone seats, 12 inches wide and 14 inches high, attached to the west, north and south walls of the nave. In the centre of the nave in the south wall, is an extremely neat Saxon arched doorway, highly ornamented, 7 feet 4 inches high, by two feet 4 inches wide. The keystone of the arch projects 8 inches on which is rudely sculptured a tyger's head. The floor was composed of sand and lime, under which bodies were unquestionably buried; the skeletons of two having been discovered. It is very remarkable that no vestige of a window can be found, unless a small aperture of inconsiderable dimensions, in the south wall of the chancel, and which is 10 feet

59

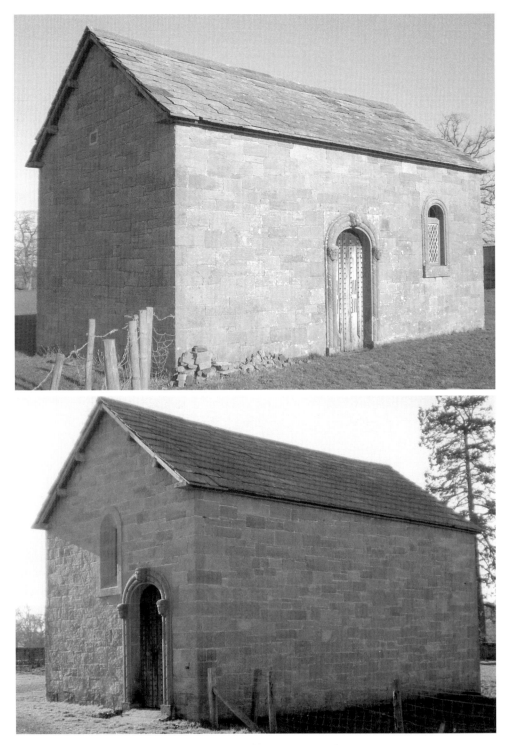

60

The Mortuary Chapel.
Opposite, top: north and
west sides.
Bottom: south and east
sides.
Right: Interior.
Below: Door on west side

61

The contrasting bearded heads on the south and east sides of the Mortuary Chapel.

above the surface of the floor, should be considered one. It must therefore be presumed that the services must have been performed by the light of tapers.

Around this interesting building lie thousands of human bones exposed to desecration; the winds having removed the sand in which they were deposited.

If this description should appear of sufficient interest to obtain a place in your columns, it is at your service for that purpose.

I am, Sir, your's very truly,

William Michell."

The discovery caused a national sensation at the time and the simple, early church resurrected from the sands had particular resonance for Sarah.

She built a small mortuary chapel that is said to be an exact copy of this offertory chapel. It is built of the same stone as St. Mary's and is 29 feet by 16 feet. The walls are 13 feet high and carry a gable roof made of Lazonby slates. The building is of slightly different proportions to the original. It is located about two hundred yards north of the church and is aligned approximately east west. There are two matching doors, one to the right of the east wall and the other at the centre of the south wall. A small arched window is placed at the centre of the east wall and a similar one on the right side in the south wall. The north and west walls are blank. Each round-arched door-frame carries the head of a man and a woman with a lion, not a "tyger", at the centre of the arch. The heads on the east wall are less sophisticated than those on the west, as though they were carved by a different person or, perhaps, as though the craftsman learnt from his initial attempts. Sarah Losh tells us that William Hindson was responsible for the palm tree that was once inside the chapel and that the female head now in the church is his. It is probable that he carved the heads above the doors. The doors, themselves, now weathered to a grey wood, are studded in imitation of medieval doors, but the studs are actually square wooden pegs. The ceiling is made from plaster lath, now seriously deteriorated. Instead of being flat it is a curious rounded construction supported by false beams made from plaster and lath. A low stone bench runs around the walls and there is a stone

altar, which, although a copy of the one in Perranzabuloe, is seriously at odds with the Anglican practice of the time. The palm tree is no longer in the chapel.

The addition of the windows, their absence a significant feature of St. Perran's, and the two human heads on each door, show the same practice of imitation and adaptation rather than copying that prompted Sarah's building.

Some yards to the west of the chapel is the graveyard. Sarah had donated this acre of land as an interdenominational burial ground some time before Katharine's death. The wall near the entrance is made of rough-hewn stones in a manner that distinguishes other work by Sarah Losh.

The Mortuary Chapel and the graveyard were consecrated on 12th May, 1842, but it is probable that they were constructed some years before - the DofE dating is 1835 - and that the Mortuary Chapel may have been the first of the public works through which Sarah may have sought to assuage her grief. A trace of her interest in the Anglo-Saxons is provided by a copy of Francis Palgrave's "History of the Anglo Saxons", which was published in 1837, and which was one of the books selected from the estate by Manchester College.

The parishioners of Wreay continued to use the extended burial ground around the old church in the area of the Losh Burial Plot, for many years.

Sarah also built a small cottage nearby for the sexton. It is a rectangular gabled structure but the original windows are round-arched and there are some smaller round arched windows as in the church.

We do not know when Sarah Losh first conceived of re-building Wreay

The Pompeian schoolhouse

church, nor when she began the preparatory work. In some ways it may have been that her life had been a preparation for this work. Her journey on the continent and much of her subsequent reading may have been preparatory, and the Mortuary Chapel and the Cross enabled her to develop her artistic and architectural abilities.

Sarah Losh left a short account of the building of the church:

"In the year 1840 the old chapel in Wreay was found to be in a very dilapidated condition, the slate was much broken, the timber of the roof was in a dangerous state of decay and the walls were in many parts mouldy and green from the moisture which trickled down them. Interments had taken place not only close to the walls, but even within them, so that in consequence of these various circumstances, the air of the building had become so vitiated as to prove injurious to the health of many of those who remained in it during the time of the service.

"A committee having been formed for the restoration of the edifice, it was resolved to apply to the proper authorities, for leave to remove to a fresh spot, where it would be unencumbered by graves. This plan was approved by the bishop and by the chancellor of the Diocese and by the Dean and Chapter of Carlisle Cathedral, who as patrons of the living agreed to give £30 to the Chancel, that being the sum estimated for replacing it exactly as it then stood. With this aid I offered to furnish a new site for the chapel and to defray all the expenses of its re-erection, on condition that I should be left unrestricted as to the mode of building it. Mrs. M. Losh and Mrs. A. Bonner both kindly gave me, the former £50, the latter £100, towards the work, and she further presented us with the coloured windows the brass eagles etc. The destruction of an ancient structure however necessary, must always afford cause for regret, but the Chapel at Wreay had apparently little claim to respect, either in an antiquarian or an architectural point of view. The state of the original chapel is supposed to be of the time of Edward 2nd; no coins were however met with when it was pulled down, to substantiate or refute this opinion. The walls were low and without any regular foundation, and although of considerable thickness, they displayed but indifferent masonry. - One

Copy of the permission granted to Miss Losh to move the road on 23rd June, 1836, from the Minute Book of the Twelve Men of Wreay Below: The crypt door

of the windows resembled the common coupled windows of the Tudor period. It had no dripstone, was of square form containing two round headed lights, the material was red sandstone rudely cut. The other windows were more modern and composed of two and three square headed lights, with coarsely hewn mullions of various sizes and proportions, while the only perceptible door was quite modern, and of miserable workmanship. In the process of demolition, however, a small narrow door was discovered near the eastern end of the south wall. It forms the entrance of the new cript and is a specimen of the flat headed corbel arch so common in the time of Edward Ist. Another doorway in a great measure broken away, was laid open in the west gable, it was much longer and had evidently constituted the principal entrance. The exterior stones had been taken away and their place supplied by ordinary walling. The interior had been coated with plaister and when this was knocked off, large projecting stones became visible, constituting a solid corbel

arch as seen in the annotated sketch made by Mr. Hindson, the builder. These discrepancies in the style of the building, added to the apparent great age of its timber, (which had clearly been worked over and differently disposed at some remote period) suggest the possibility that the late chapel had been built at a time comparatively recent, from the remains of an original edifice, of which the western doorway and part of the gable may have been left standing, but marred and spoilt by unskillful hands.

"On clearing the ground for the present chapel, the workmen discovered at no great depth, a series of broad, thick, white flagstones, forming two

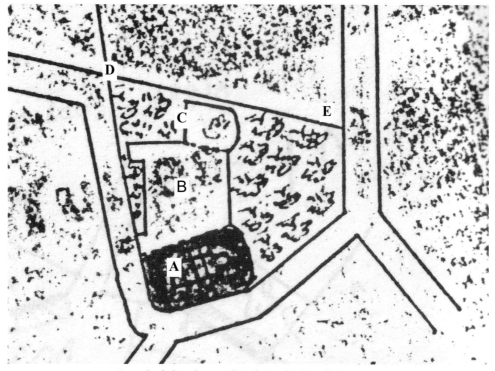

Detail of the plan in Sarah Losh's hand showing:
the proposed location of the new church (A), with the outlines of the walls; the old grave-
yard and the site of the old church (B); the proposed extension to the graveyard which ap-
pears to be on the site of the Cross (C) and the line of the old road (D-E).

angles of a considerable building, of which no other trace has been left. It is possible that a square tower may have anciently occupied this place, adjoining to which is a field still denominated the guards. Some sort of defence must have been required at a manufacturing village, as Wreay formerly was, especially exposed to aggression by its proximity to Inglewood Forest, the noted retreat of desperate outlaws. There was indeed a tower or constable house, till recently standing in Wreay Hall, where it would form protection to the Potteries on the banks of the Petteril, but there is no reason from hence to infer that no other tower subsisted in the vicinity, and it was not unlikely that such should be placed at Wreay, as the intermediate station between Carlisle and Melguards, as this latter was the middle post betwixt Carlisle and Penrith. Some persons may conjecture that the foundation in question had been that of some cell or other edifice connected with the chapel, but of such there is no record, on the contrary it is an established fact that a monthly service was performed there by one of the monks of St. Mary's Abbey which

66

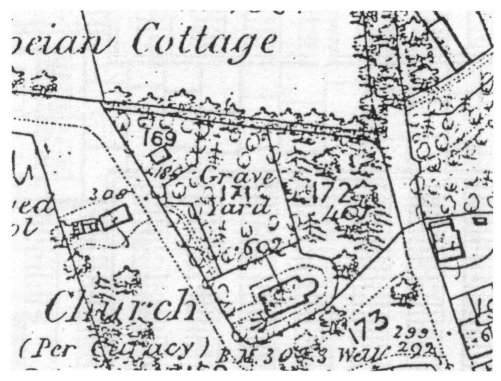

The same area as depicted on the first edition of the OS map.

owned the tythes of the Chapelry, it seemed prior to the consecration by Bishop Fleming, for a school also. These foundations were lifted and afterwards replaced at a greater depth, but nearly in the same direction, for the groundwork (as far as they extended) of the present chapel - one small flag only being taken away and laid as a specimen of the rest, at the schoolmaster's gate. The plot of ground on which the chapel now stands was anciently part of the common belonging to the Township, by the proprietors of which, on the enclosure of Wreay Common, it was hedged in to form a cow grassing for the clerk. This outer enclosure formed an irregular belt of more or less breadth surrounding the chapel yard on every side. It was made over to me by the Township in 1836, in exchange for another piece of land for the clerk, thus enabling me to improve the appearance of the place by planting it with evergreens and also to rebuild. with a little additional space, the wall of the chapel yard, which had almost wholly disappeared - subsequently it gave me the means of affording a new site for the chapel. The ground was very uneven and had formerly several pools of water, on which, when frozen, the schoolboys skated. On levelling the water gushed up and filled the new-dug foundation so rapidly, that it was necessary to fill it with stones, and to commence further to the eastward. This water was drained off at a low level, and conveyed underneath the chapel floor, in a large drain through the cript, where it receives the water from the shallow drains made outside the chapel walls. From the cript the large drain takes a north easterly direction across the outer garth where it is joined by the main drain from the new and old part of the Chapel yard. After this it is carried underneath the public road and thro' the orchard opposite, whence there is a good descent for it down the bank. To secure the dryness of the chapel floor the flags are raised on dwarf walls, with the exception of the platform at the entrance which is raised on dry stone chippings. In order to dispense with spouts the roof of the chapel projects well over the walls, the emblematical monsters which are placed like gargoyles, being meant for ventilators, or for the emission of smoke. The Dragon which serves for the latter purpose, is not like the others poised properly on the wall; the projecting part being too ponderous, so that it is kept in its place mainly by the stones above it. Should any repairs be required there, great caution should be used to prevent its falling. The iron bar inserted in its jaw, is to prevent the starlings from making nests in it. A fine brood of young birds was hatched there soon after its erection, and the flue was completely choked up by the sticks and rubbish of the nest.

"Some caution will be needed in repairing such of the windows as are made of alabaster which is exceptionally brittle. The walls of the Chapel have been coated not with plaister but with Roman cement. This is a superior covering if not broken into, but its liability to crack unfits it for any wall designed for the reception of monumental tablets. These I would earnestly hope would not be introduced into this rustic chapel, the simplicity and uniformity of which, would be totally destroyed, by the glaring aspect of black, white or coloured marble, with the usual decorations either heraldic or mortuary. Indeed I would hope the time is not distant, when Christians will have too much reverence for their places of worship, to fill them with memorials of their dead, and that the pernicious practice of interment within these sacred buildings, will soon be entirely abandoned. No interments can properly take place nearer to the Chapel at Wreay than the boundary line of the original chapel yard. The narrow raised strip of ground on the south side of the chapel yard, had been added to it by me, when the wall was rebuilt, but has not been used nor consecrated, and on the erection of the new chapel, it was deemed advizeable by Mr. Jackson to restore the former line of boundary on this side, in order to keep the burial ground more distant from the building, and with his consent, 1 therefore had walled in, a square piece of ground on the north side of the chapel yard, in exchange for this narrow strip. The square

South east view of the old church dated 12th July 1836, by the Rev. W. Ford.

plot contains more superficial feet of space than the other - it has been raised, levelled and drained most carefully, and was consecrated along with the chapel in 1842. The strip of ground was left purposely without consecration and has been planted with low growing shrubs. With regard to the old materials of the fabric, the stones and flags were by agreement used up by the builder, and the only window in tolerable repair (which the chapelry inserted a few years since) was set aside to be employed at the parsonage; the others were used as common stones and some of the timber was laid as sleepers for the seats, some applied to other purposes, but it was of little value, the spars were indeed so much decayed as to be taken for firewood by the workmen who required large fires within and without the building. The old pews were interspersed behind the slates and the wood ceiling, the pulpit and reading desk fell to pieces with age and dampness and were quite useless. The communion table is preserved in the cript.

"Some of the slates were taken for different purposes in the course of the work for drains etc. and a few are still left. The bell gable has been placed by the pond at the roadside to remain as a relic of the former chapel. The old glass was so much shattered that it was valued at 14 shillings, which amount the glazier deducted from his bill.

"The unpolished mode of building adhered to in the new chapel, most approximates to early Saxon or modified Lombard, which was preferred to a more improved style, as less expensive and elaborate. In conformity to this primitive manner of building, large windows could not have been made in the absis, but the Bishop fearing a want of light, gave only a conditional assent to the plan as it now stands, desiring that it should be so contrived that larger windows might be opened if found desirable. These, however, he afterwards dispensed with. The alabaster is cut to represent different aspects of the fossil flora chiefly found in Northumberland and Durham.

"Inside of the old Chapel doorway only visible on removing the plaister. The outside was totally defaced." This last note accompanies a ground plan of doorway copied from Mr Hindson's sketch.

The above is a copy of a transcript made by the Rev. Jackson of a document in Sarah Losh's own hand. Hall extracts some points from the document and simply refers to it as an account or memorandum without explaining why it was written and for whom.

To have such a memorandum derived from Sarah Losh's own hand is intensely interesting. The "early Saxon or modified Lombard" were "preferred to a more improved style, as less expensive and elaborate". This seems a disingenuous statement on her part. She had been offered thirty pounds by the church authorities which was deemed the cost of replacing the earlier chancel. She chose to spend £1,088 10s. 4d, thirty-six times as much, and then suggests that the design was determined by the need for economy. For comparison, a year later, Sarah provided most of the £800 for the restoration and extension of St. John the Baptist in Newton Arlosh. The extension alone is far larger than the church at Wreay and the work was done in conformity with much normal practice of the time in a standard Anglo-Norman style.

The veil that is drawn over the disagreement with the bishop might hide a great deal. Although Bishop Hugh Percy belonged to a very broad church and stood aside from the earnest doctrinal debates of the day, he must have had concerns about the Losh design. Percy may have taken a great interest in restoring the Bishop's Palace at nearby Rose Castle and been a wealthy aristocrat and keen horseman, but he was also the son-in-law of an Archbishop of Canterbury. His view that the apse should be well lit is probably not just utilitarian. Wreay is

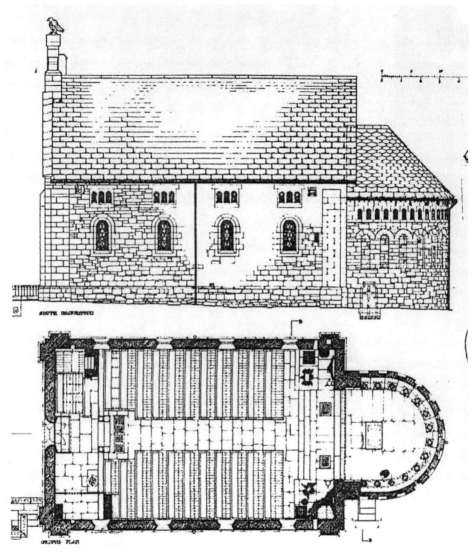

A plan of the church and south section drawn by John Robinson.

peculiar in the dimness of its lighting - something remarked on by early commentators - and this, coupled with the unorthodox positioning of the illegal communion table or, more properly, altar, since it was made of stone, and the lotus candlesticks, must have tested the Bishop's Anglican tolerance. Lonsdale is scathing, suggesting that the established church had been hoodwinked: "the significance of which was hardly comprehended by Bishop Percy and his episcopate supporters assembled on the day of its consecration". One wonders by what process a woman, albeit a

71

very wealthy, intelligent and determined woman, was able to prevail against the forces of the Church of England. The sentence: "These, however, he afterwards dispensed with," is probably cutting a long story far too short. Sarah Losh had stipulated that the finance was "on condition that I should be left unrestricted as to the mode of building it".

Sarah was immensely practical, terse and to-the-point in her description of the technical issues - she knew what she was doing. She was keen to demonstrate the re-use of materials, interested and perceptive on historical and archaeological issues and alive to the world around her. Notice the pictures of the schoolboys skating and the "fine brood of young chicks" in the dragon chimney.

The passage that tells us most about her religious thinking is the one about church burials and memorials: "The walls of the Chapel have been coated not with plaister but with Roman cement. This is a superior covering if not broken into, but its liability to crack unfits it for any wall designed for the reception of monumental tablets. These I would earnestly hope would not be introduced into this rustic chapel, the simplicity and uniformity of which, would be totally destroyed, by the glaring aspect of black, white or coloured marble, with the usual decorations either heraldic or mortuary. Indeed I would hope the time is not distant, when Christians will have too much reverence for their places of worship, to fill them with memorials of their dead, and that the pernicious practice of interment within these sacred buildings, will soon be entirely abandoned". A practical, carefully gauged point about the impracticality of monuments on the Roman cement is followed by a concern for the chapel's aesthetic: the monuments would destroy "the simplicity and uniformity" of this rustic chapel. But the issue is neither the practical one of the cement nor the aesthetic one of harmony but her strong feeling that images of death do not belong in a place of worship. This is her most forceful verbal statement and has a significant bearing on her church which is overflowing with images of life.

What she does not comment on, except for the practical reference to the fossils in the alabaster windows, is the imagery.

Sarah Losh also explains the sequence of preparation. Land had been donated, the road diverted, a graveyard moved and all the necessary administrative procedures had been followed. The work must have taken its first practical step when Sarah Losh applied to the Twelve Men of Wreay, a village council of some antiquity, to divert the road that followed the line of Chapel Hill to the north and east of the present church to join the Carlisle Road opposite Wreay Sike. They gave their permission on the 20th June, 1836.

The Faculty to rebuild Wreay Chapel was granted on 20th May, 1841. It gives permission to "take down the present fabric of the Chapel of Wreay aforesaid and the Chancel thereof and to erect a new and more commodious structure in lieu thereof upon or within the distance of thirty yards from the present site thereof as may be judged expedient and to complete perfect and finish the said intended new Chapel and Chancel so as to make and render the same fit and convenient for the celebration of Divine Service and hearing sermons therein and further to do and perform all other acts matters and things requisite and necessary for taking down rebuilding finishing and completing the same".

Five days later, on 25th May, Sarah Losh wrote to the "Carlisle Journal" insisting that her intention was not to erect a new church but simply to "re-edify the old Chapel". the actual letter runs as follows:

"To the Editor of the Carlisle Journal

Miss Losh will be much obliged to the Editor of the Carlisle Journal if he will rectify a statement which appeared in his last paper, respecting a building commenced at Wreay; at which place it is not intended to erect a Church, but merely to re-edify the old Chapel.

Although regretting to call attention to so trivial an undertaking, she considers it due to the various parties, who are concerned most, to place the affair in its right point of view. The expense of replacing the seats &c, will be defrayed by the Chapelry at large. The Dean and Chapter of Carlisle (who are the Patrons of the living) gave thirty pounds for the construction of the Church, for the rest, she has been kindly assisted by some of her own relations.

On the occasion of laying the first stone of this rustic structure, an appropriate prayer was offered by the Rev. R. Jackson; and some coins were deposited in the foundation by the hands of his infant son.

Woodside, Tuesday, May 25th."

That very day a vestry committee had appointed a sub-committee to supervise the building that required a quorum of three. From the little information we have, we might presume that Sarah Losh was wanting to keep her plans as low key as possible until she was sure she had full control of the project. It appears she was quite prepared to make economies with the truth to obtain her ends.

At that vestry committee meeting Sarah Losh so arranged things that with the support of the Rev. Richard Jackson and the churchwarden, she would have control. That first committee had its mundane concerns and appears to lack vision and ambition:

"At a vestry meeting of the Chapelry and Township of Wreay held this day in pursuance of legal notice

<u>Resolved unanimously</u>

that the kind proposal made by Miss Losh to rebuild the Chapel at Wreay be accepted.

That all the seats be made single to face the Reading Desk.

That these be all made of yellow pine & instead of doors have a piece of wood fixed to one end of the back of the seats with a little ornament on the top such as may be agreed to by the committee.

that the following committee be authorized to make arrangements for carrying these resolutions into effect, & transact any business connected with the new chapel viz.- Sarah Losh; Richard Jackson; James Longrigg, Chapelwarden; John Robinson, Scalesceugh; Thomas Slack; William Carrick; Joseph Scott and three to form a quorum.

that a seat for the singers, another for the schoolmaster & clerk's family, and the same number of sittings as at present be filled up & the expense borne by the owners of the respective seats according to the number of sittings.

that the expense assigned to Miss Losh be borne by the other owners

that Miss Losh put up her own seat & free sittings

that the expense of consecrating the chapel be defrayed in the general account as above.

that the thanks of the meeting be given to Miss Losh for her very generous and liberal offer to rebuild the Chapel.

that the seats be painted

Present at this meeting - Richard Jackson, minister & chairman; James Longrigg, Chapel Warden; John Robinson, Scalesceugh; Thomas Slack, Intack; Joseph Scott; William Carrick; John Pearson, Park; Wm. S Moffit for Joseph Sewell; Robert Lamb; William Longrigg; John Squires; William Strong; Joseph Carr for Charles Graham; William Lancaster; John Farish".

The Committee are properly grateful to Miss Losh. They want their church plain and simple - pews of painted pine - and want to ensure the requisite social allocation and payments and they envisage the Reading Desk, and thus the Scriptures, being at the focal point of their worship. But there is talk only of rebuilding the Chapel.

By the end of the summer, on 1st September, Miss Losh is clearly in charge. The committee's ambitions have been raised, the best and appropriate foreign timbers are to be used, the oak and flooring timber coming from the far reaches of the Baltic, and somebody is clearly paying close attention to technical specifications.

"September 1st 1841

At a meeting of the Committee for re-building the Chapel at Wreay

It was unanimously resolved

that the framing of the panels for the seats be of the best Danzig oak and that Spanish chesnut be used for the Pannels, Newel posts and seats.

that the floor of the seats be laid with Memel boards of 1 inch in thickness on oak sleepers -

and Miss Losh & Revd. Jackson have the liberty of making any alteration respecting the choice of wood, and that they determine the dimensions & width of the seats - and any other matters respecting the Chapel

Richard Jackson, Chairman; John Robinson; William Carrick; Joseph Scott; Thomas Slack"

That final throwaway phrase giving Miss Losh and Revd. Jackson authority over "any other matter respecting the Chapel" reveals Sarah Losh's determination to have complete control over the building.

It is also possible that the long discourse on the drainage problems in Sarah Losh's memorandum is a justification for moving the site of the Chapel and thereby building a totally new structure. It would be very interesting to discover what was really happening in this Trollopean process.

The finances show the same gathering of the reins into her hands:

"An Account of money received and expended for rebuilding and enlarging The Chapel at Wreay in the Parish of St. Mary's, Carlisle.

Subscriptions received

Dean & Chapter of Carlisle	30	0	0
Miss Ann Bonner, Brisco Cottage	145	0	0
Miss Margaret Losh, Woodside	100	0	0
Miss Losh, Woodside	815	14	4

The total came to £1090 14 4 and for all practical purposes the monies were there for Sarah Losh to spend on the Church as she determined. The Dean and Chapter's £30 was the (probably) reasonable sum for the repair of a small rural chapel that had been built a hundred years before. As corporate rector their responsibility was for the maintenance of only the chancel of the new church, as it had been of the old one. It was just two and a half per cent of the final cost of the new church and suggests that the church accepted the complete control that Sarah Losh had asked for. The £245 from Sarah's aunts was at her disposal, and may have been contributed because Sarah did not have limitless ready funds to pay for everything outright herself.

The Document of Consecration of Wreay Chapel was issued on 1st December, 1842. The church was built in the remarkably short time of eighteen months. The problems faced with the water and the foundations and the false start which required a re-location must have made for an even tighter schedule. Such expedition is even more remarkable since the work was done by local tradesmen working on an unfamiliar project under the direction of an inexperienced and amateur architect and producing work to a demanding specification in unfamiliar materials such as the Roman cement.

We are fortunate in having a full list of payments made for the Church. Like the memorandum, and the above documents, this was found amongst the Rev. Richard Jackson's possessions and copied out and sent on to Canon Hall from whence it now reposes in Carlisle Archives:

"Wreay Chapel & Chapel yard 1841, 1842	£	S	D
Bulman waggoner	3	4	3
Labourers' wages	40	2	4
cartage	6	5	0
W Hindson mason work & materials	349	7	1
W Hindson 2nd bill	6	5	0
W Hindson 3rd bill	5	13	9
W Hindson junior	19	11	0
W Hindson junior	9	10	8
Robinson for stones (3 Bills)	16	19	10
Stone from Shawk quarry	7	5	5½
Slate & flags from Lazonby	33	13	0
Stones Lazonby		16	0
Slating	14	9	8
Harrison for nails (3 bills)	14	14	10
D Robinson iron work	5	11	7
J Scott iron work	10	11	3
Botchergate foundry		10	0
Lead Mrs Lawrie	3	12	11
Roman cement (Nelson's yard)	4	9	4
Glendinning whitesmith	5	18	0
copper nails		11	0
Sagurs foundery		14	0
Cement from Newcastle	12	12	0
carriage thereof	1	4	0
Anderson plaistering 999	22	9	8
Wailes for Windows	42	16	8
Rowell Glazier (after deducting 14s for old Chap. windows)	9	1	9½
Lock &c for Chapel door		9	7
Font dish	1	5	0

glass for font		14	6
Binnell for oil	2	18	10
J Macdonald joiners work	111	11	9
Scott & partner sawing	31	10	10
Walker for Memel timber	32	10	11
Walker American elm	13	15	0
Walker additional elm	1	12	1
sawing it		16	0
Stephenson joiners work		9	2
larch & sawing it at sawmill for flooring	4	0	0
Oak wood cut at Woodbank & Woodside say	150	0	0
J Macdonalds contract for such	20	0	0
Scott sawing for ditto	1	7	0
Scott sawing for ditto	8	18	0
Richardson Chesnut wood for seats	28	7	0
Nicholson (Annan) dantzig oak	13	6	9
Loading Dantzig oak at Woodside sawmill		4	0
Loading chesnut wood from Carlisle	1	16	0
Advertizing work		4	6
Horsing planks		1	0
Moving old seats		8	9
Chesnut wood for carving	2	4	0
Scott carving eagle & carriage thereof	5	1	6
Scott for Stork	5	0	0
Scott for other carving	2	4	0
Stone eagle	2	1	6
Black oak - expense of getting from the Moss	1	10	0
total	1092	7	4
for chesnut slabs remaining valued at £1.1.0 & 6 bits of Dantzig			
Oak valued at 12 shillings deduct.	1	13	0
remains total sum	1090	14	4
for sale of old oak etc	1	10	0
	1089	4	4
Rowell for old windows		14	0

There are some other things the cost of which cannot be well ascertained & which it is not necessary to charge. The principal of these are alabaster for windows and font

Stephenson's work in sawing alabaster

Alabaster hair for plaister for chancel - draining tiles, brass wire & cord - chair & deal face lamps & 2 ebony panels from Paris

Stove ornaments from Paris

Books & binding in wood

Sundries - wear and tear of carts, barrow ropes & scaffold bands

additional labour

Stephenson assisting

Robert Donald carving

additional railway carriage

talk(talc) for windows & cutting it

N.B. Some deduction should have been made from the bills of Wm Hindson Junior, as they included the oratory palm tree & poor Smallwood's monument; but to set against these, there is the female head in the chancel arch, which he finished and was paid for, some years since for a different purpose, & which in intrinsic value may fully outweigh them - the wood cut at Woodbank & Woodside I believe to be set down considerably below its value. There is no charge made for the site of the chapel, wood for stork & eagle & Mr Richardson".

The work was carried out by William Hindson, a member of a local family from the nearby hamlet of Mellguards. The Hindsons had been stonemasons for several generations. In "Mannix and Whellan's Directory" William Hindson is listed as being a farmer as well. It is almost certain that this small rural church was one of the largest and most demanding works he had been employed on. The total money he received was £361.5s.10d, but this included materials as well as labour. The going-rate for basic unskilled labour, according to another set of accounts for clearing the village green, was one shilling a day, with some named workers earning as much as 2s.4d. One hundred pounds would purchase between a thousand and two thousand man-days depending on the skill of the worker. Hindson's responsibility for materials suggests that the stone was quarried locally. Many houses, walls and gate-posts in the immediate parish are of the same yellow/grey sandstone, whereas ones further afield are in a red sandstone which is far more common in the area.

The stone supplied by the Shawk Quarry is probably the lighter uniform stone used in the apse. The quarry may also be the source of the durable, clean-edged stone used for the carved windows and doorway. Shawk foot or Shalkfoot, at Cumdivock about ten miles west of Wreay, had been quarried since Roman times and was used for building Carlisle city walls and Carlisle Cathedral. Mannix and Whellan discuss the quarry as follows: "On its rugged and rocky banks are chalk quarries, where three different beds of stone are wrought, viz., one of red free stone, of an open grit; another of very white free stone, of a close body; and a seam of limestone".

Lazonby slates and flags were used on the roof and came from a quarry about a dozen miles to the south-east. Lazonby flags were red-sandstone flagstones and are still to be seen on the roofs of some older farmhouses in the area. They were an unusual choice at this date. They are a heavy form of roofing and had largely been replaced by slate from Borrowdale or elsewhere in the Lake District.

The Roman cement which Sarah Losh used, unusually on the interior of the building, made a quick-setting mortar which formed a hard, stone-like surface. It was the patented product of James Parker and was obtained from the marble works of Thomas and James Nelson in Carlisle.

She paid William Wailes of Newcastle £42.16.8 for the stained glass windows. Wailes had been a tea merchant and grocer, but he had a passion for medieval glass, sold his grocery business to his partner and set up as a stained glass manufacturer in 1841. Sarah Losh, with her unusual and very specific demands, must have been amongst his earliest clients. Later he became one of the country's leading stained glass manufacturers and was Augustus Pugin's principal supplier. Geoffrey Rowell of Grey Coat Lane in Carlisle would have been responsible for the other glazing work, including the protective glass over the alabaster windows.

Well over £400 was spent on wood and joinery. Most of the bought timber was obtained from Carlisle merchants. Walkers, who supplied the American elm and Memel timber, had a yard in West Tower Street, in the centre of Carlisle, and Richardsons were in St. Nicholas's to the south-east of the city. If Lonsdale's reference to the use of Spanish chestnut from trees brought down in gales at Lowther Park is correct, then Richardson's must have acted as the merchants. The Dantzig oak, used in the seats with the chestnut, may well have been a special order as it was obtained through a shipping firm in Annan which was over thirty miles away.

In some ways the use of oak from the estates at Woodside and Woodhouses is surprising. The under-estimated valuation of the oak at £150 represents a considerable amount of timber. Under a hundred pounds was spent in purchasing all the other timber for the church. Sarah and Katharine had been very involved in the development of their estate and the scale of the tree felling involved, even if thinning was needed, would have had some visual impact. It may have been a way of economising or it may have been that Sarah felt that there was a resonance in using her own timber grown on her ancestral estate to build a church that had such personal significance.

There was much voluntary labour. For instance, on June 14th, four men - Pickering from Bridge End; David Robinson; Mr. Robinson and Tom Longrigg - volunteered and five men provided carts: Mr Wm Slack lent two carts; George Brown,Thomas Morley, and George Graham, all from Foulbridge, lent one each. Two days later, on 16th June, there were five volunteers: Henry Gill of Little Barrock, William Birbeck of Burnthwaite, Mr T. Slack of Intack, James Longrigg and William Porter.

John Scott, a cripple who lived at Dalston, was responsible for the carvings of the stork and eagle lecterns. He charged five pounds each for these fine birds, but there is an additional payment of £2.4.0. This may have been for the two archangels, which are similar in style, the feathering of the wings, for instance, but it is hardly a proportionate payment. It is possible that he added the wings and the lily and palm to two already existing figures. The figures themselves are very human in their portrayal. Alternatively, the payment might have been for the figures above the chancel arch or for the owl and the cockerel.

The inclusion of "Robert Donald carving" among the sundries refers to a Robert Donald whose entry in "Mannix and Whelan" is unusually precise: "gardener to Miss Losh"; and thereby concurs with Lonsdale's statement that Miss Losh's gardener was responsible for the sinuous carving of the gourd plant around the doorframe.

William Hindson, Junior, was paid a total of £29.1.8 for the stone carving. A footnote explains payment for "the oratory palm tree & poor Smallwood's monument", - Smallwood had been killed in a tree-felling accident - was included in the payment for the work on the church. However, "there is the female head in the chancel arch, which he finished and was paid for, some years since for a different purpose, & which in intrinsic value may fully outweigh them". The fact that this very accomplished piece of work was done "some years since" suggests that Hindson had been carving stone for some time. The female head is similar to the two on the Mortuary Chapel and it is possible to see an artistic progression through all three. Hindson may have been sent to Italy for instruction, as Hall suggests, and the prevalence of such a strong local anecdote probably confirms its partial truth, but it is probable that he was already a very skilful craftsman when he made his journey. Hindson will have carved the windows and doors on the west end and the heads on the chancel arch. The quality of the carving on the pillar capitals in the apse is not good enough to be his work.

There is no mention in the costings of the painting on the walls of the apse. The quality of the painting, its artistic freedom and its originality coupled with a naivete in some of the execution such as the proportions of the lamb, suggest that this is not the work of a trained professional. It is possible that the images at the heart of the church were painted by Sarah Losh herself.

We know that she did carve the sides of the font herself and this work shows a very high level of craftsmanship in the fashioning of an unforgiving material.

Her cousin, William Septimus Losh, the youngest of James's sons, carved the alabaster lotus flowers and water-lilies that are on the font cover. He may have helped elsewhere. He was 24 years younger than Sarah and had married his first cousin, Sarah Spencer, daughter of George Losh, on 21st May, 1831, at the British Embassy Chapel, Paris. He brought the fragments of medieval glass back from Paris. He built Wreay Syke, a large house just across the road from the east end of the church that has some features of Sarah Losh's architectural style. He and his wife are buried in the Losh Burial Enclosure. Their gravestones are in an elaborate medieval style.

The account mentions no fee for an architect. There is no doubt that Sarah Losh was responsible for the conception of the building. We do not know how she put this concept into execution. No drawings have been found and there are no accounts of her working methods apart from the references to drawing and modelling to be imitated by the craftsmen. Given the unusual nature of the building and her very specific requirements, the high level of technical awareness she shows in the memorandum, the precise detailing of the accounts and her considerable knowledge of mathematics and scientific and technical matters and the firmness and decisiveness of her character, Sarah Losh must have exercised a high level of close control over the project. She will have drawn architectural plans and will have supervised the work closely.

When a building departs so far from tradition and normal practice as Wreay Church, it is tempting to look for specific sources and influences. Sarah Losh's work is a radical departure from all other contemporary building. Pevsner draws attention to a German revival of Lombardic style building of which she would not have been aware, and to several near contemporary English buildings which she anticipates.

The interest in Italian building fostered by her "grand tour" and the broad acquaintance with early Italian churches indicated by Lonsdale were probably enough to prompt Sarah Losh's original imagination. She was a grand eclectic, willing and ready to take what she wanted, where she wanted, and use it to her own purpose. Her work, the Cross, the Mortuary Chapel, the Losh Burial Plot, the Mausoleum, the Church and even the houses - the Pompeian court at Woodside, the Pompeian Cottage - had always imitated and adapted the antique. There was little pattern or consistency in this borrowing - the sophis-

Elevations of San Michele, Pavia, and the Duomo in Parma from Thomas Hope's "An Historical Essay on Architecture".

tication of the Bewcastle Cross is far removed from the simplicity of St. Perran's. The Mausoleum combines the cyclopeian walls of an imagined Homeric Greece with a contemporary romantic statue and does so successfully because of their poetic sympathy. The Mortuary windows have Norman decoration, the archaic-style graves have Italian balustrading. She was ready to use anything with which she had a sympathy. This sympathy may have been personal, a detail or feature which simply appealed or had acquired an association, or spiritual because it expressed a sense of another time and place and sensibility, or philosophical because of its cultural and historical significance. Sarah Losh was not part of any movement.

The apse of St Leonard's Church, Warwick on Eden, and the Font at Bridekirk.

An engraving of the east end of St Leonard's Church, Warwick on Eden, from Jefferson's "Carlisle".

However, in 1835 a book was published which might have had some influence on her choice of structure. Bullen and Drew both suggest that Thomas Hope's posthumously published, "An Historical Essay on Architecture illustrated from Drawings made by him in Italy and Germany" offered some contemporary exemplars for Wreay. The works illustrated are large duomos and could not serve as models for St. Mary's although they offer motifs, such as the stepped arcade of small windows. I suspect Sarah Losh's real sources are to be found in the sketchbooks she kept on her continental tour.

The Church of St. Leonard in nearby Warwick on Eden, where Sarah's maternal relatives, The Warwicks, lived, could well have suggested the shape of the apse. A contemporary account, 1838, of "The History and Antiquities of Carlisle" by an inveterate city author, publisher and bookseller, Thomas Jefferson, prints an engraving that displays marked similarities to Wreay Church. The brief commentary suggests further parallels: "Near Warwick Hall, is the curious church of St. Leonard, which is of Norman origin, erected probably before the conquest; and has an apsis or semicircular east end - a form comparatively rare in England. On the exterior, this semicircular termination of the chancel of the church, has thirteen narrow niches, measuring ten feet eight inches high, and one foot five inches broad, reaching almost to the ground; three of them have small windows inserted. These were intended to signify Christ and his twelve apostles. The whole structure is about twenty-four yards in length, but once extended twenty-one feet further west, which space was occupied by a tower; the interior arch, evidently a Norman one, alone remains." The church was considerably remodelled in the 1870s, but the Norman apse is still there, though much restored.

In the same way, she may have derived the concept of a decorated font from the very beautiful, but very different, twelfth century font in Bridekirk Church, near Cockermouth. Her friend, Henry Howard, made drawings of the font in addition to those he made of the Cross at Bewcastle.

Sarah will have heard of the death of William Thain sometime in the early part of 1842, when the structural work of the church must have been well advanced. He was a major with the 21st Foot, serving as aide de camp to the incompetent General Elphinstone, and was killed in action in the disastrous massacre of the Jugdullak Pass (the Pass of Coord Cabul) in the Afghan Wars. For many years a pine tree stood beside the Losh Burial Plot with a stone bearing an inscription which read: "This Khelat Pine is planted in memory of Wm. Thain, Major of the 33rd, and was raised from seed transmitted by him to England. He perished in the fatal Pass of Coord Cabul, esteemed and lamented by all who knew him." He had, in fact, been in 33rd Foot Regiment 27 years earlier when he was wounded at Waterloo.

Thain was about ten years younger than Sarah, came from a Newcastle family who were on friendly terms with her Uncle James, and had been sent to school in Wreay when he was a young boy. Over the years a legend has developed suggesting an attachment between either Sarah or Katharine and Thain. This legend is felt sufficient by some sentimental souls to account for the pine imagery and the arrows in the church. A romantic attachment seems unlikely. Sarah and Katharine were significantly older than Thain when he was living on the Bewley farm in Wreay. In later years he followed an active military career. If there had been a romantic attachment there would probably have been no social obstacles to marriage. Neither Thain nor the Losh sisters married. John Losh, who is the only person who might have raised an objection to a marriage, died in 1814 when Thain was 18. Sarah's dedication, "esteemed and lamented" is cold and informal when compared to the ones to her sister and parents and gives no hint of any special affection. It is also inconceivable that she would not have known that he was in the 21st Foot and not the 33rd if she had continued a close acquaintance with him. Thain sent the cone as a gift, no doubt because of Sarah's enthusiasm for planting many and various trees. It would be surprising if the use of the cone imagery in the church had not already been determined by the time she heard of his death.

On the other hand, it is difficult to explain the use of arrows, and especially the one driven into the chancel wall, other than by reference to Thain. The use of the cones must have acquired a special resonance because of the death of a childhood friend. Similarly the brutal death in the course of duty of someone she had known as a little boy must have touched her deeply as she worked on the church and might have prompted this crude, dramatic and despairing symbol of death in a church where she felt there should be no memorials to death.

The well just to the right of the church door has railings made of downward pointing arrows buried in the ground. (The present, badly-cast arrows have replaced the earlier well-fashioned ones.) These arrows may also be associated with Thain's death.

St Mary's Church, Wreay, was consecrated by Bishop Percy on 1st December, 1842. The report in the "Carlisle Patriot" on the following day gave this account of the proceedings:

"December 1st 1842

Consecration of New Chapel

The interesting ceremony of the consecration of the new chapel took place on Thursday December 1st 1842. The doors were opened at ten o'clock, & very shortly afterwards the area of this exceedingly handsome structure was crowded with the elite of Carlisle & the neighbourhood.

The Revd. R Jackson, the incumbent, was upon this occasion supported by the presence of a numerous body of the neighbouring Clergy, who awaited at the Parsonage House, the arrival of his Lordship the Bishop of Carlisle.

At eleven o'clock, his Lordship and the Chaplain, Revd. Chancellor Fletcher, were received at the West Door. The petition for Consecration was then read by Mr. Mounsey, and having been acceded to by the Bishop, His Lordship proceeded to the Altar, reading alternately with the clergy the 24th Psalm. His Lordship then took his place on the north side of the Altar – The Very Reverend, the Dean of Carlisle, the Revd. the Chancellor on the south side, the rest of the clergy being seated in the front of the congregation. The proper dedicatory Prayers and Collects were then read by the Bishop, after which the sentence of Consecration was proclaimed by the Chancellor, signed by the Bishop, and given by his Lordship to Mr Mounsey, the Registrar for Enrollment.

The service of the morning was then read by the Revd. Jackson, the Jubilate, the 26th and the 100th Psalms being sung remarkably well by the Choir of the Chapel. The Sermon, a highly impressive and forcible Discourse, forming a running commentary on the beautiful first Lesson of the Day, 1st Kings Chap VIII from 22nd to 62nd verse, was preached by his Lordship the Bishop of Carlisle.

85

After the service of the morning prayer was concluded, the Bishop and his Clergy accompanied by the Choir, repaired to the new portion of the Burial ground which was about to be consecrated. The Customary Prayers were then read by the Bishop, and the choir sung a part of the 39th Psalm.

A sumptuous collation was provided at Woodside, whither the Clergy repaired after the conclusion of the Services of the day.

The weather was propitious and the scene at Wreay was very animating. The whole arrangements displayed great care & judgment; and we understand the Bishop expressed his appreciation of the admirable manner in which all things had been prepared and made ready for this interesting service.

Among the Clergy present we noticed the Revd. Messrs Heysham, Wilkinson, Salkeld, Twentyman, Kitchen, Thwaytes, Hudson, Thomlinson, Wood, Hilton, Gibson, Brown. Etc. etc.

Altho we are aware that the unobtrusive and truly Christian Character of the Lady's benevolence, makes her prefer to do good by stealth, it is only right to add that the inhabitants are wholly indebted to the munificent liberality of Miss Losh, of Woodside, for the Erection of this Elegant and convenient place of worship".

The journalist's report gives nothing away. There is a very similar account of the consecration of St. John's Church in Stanwix in the same year. It would have been extremely interesting to know how the Bishop, the Clergy and the congregation responded to "this Elegant and convenient place of worship".

In 1843 Sarah Losh part-financed, along with Canon Simpson of Holme Cultram Abbey and others, the restoration and extension of St. John the Baptist's Church in Newton Arlosh. Newton Arlosh, once a medieval market town founded in the early fourteenth century after the floods which destroyed Skinburness, was understood to be the place of origin of the Losh family. The church was one of those strongly fortified buildings to be seen on the Solway Plain which served as defensive retreats for people and animals when faced with the incursions of the maurauding Scots.

The church was changed again in 1894, when an altar was brought from the Church of St. Paul in Carlisle and placed against the north wall. The apse was enclosed and made into a vestry. There are few signs of Sarah Losh's hand in the church. The present apse is brightly lit; there are two carved ram's heads on the east wall, a wooden eagle and two stools made from bog oak and a stone eagle on the east gable.

The Losh Burial Enclosure in Wreay was probably constructed at this time. The enclosure was originally surrounded by the graves of other parishioners and it is only in recent years that it has stood alone. The balustrade continues the

Newton Arlosh Church.
Left: the apse. Below:
ram's head shelf and the
eagle on the roof.

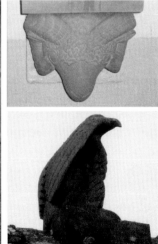

The stone that Sarah Losh placed over her parents's' grave.

repeated small arched pattern of the small rounded windows found in the church and the houses and on Katharine's Well. The plot is approximately rectangular apart from a small square cut oddly out of the north-east corner.

The graves are extra-ordinary. In an age and of a class where opulent and ostentatious tombs were expected, the Losh graves have a ponderous simplicity. The grave of John and Isabella Losh is a rough-hewn block of sandstone, perhaps three feet by two feet, smoothed on the south side only where it bears the following inscription:

> "HERE WERE LAID THE REMAINS OF JOHN LOSH OF
> WOODSIDE WHO DIED MARCH 31ST AD 1814 AGED 59
> AND OF ISABELLA HIS WIFE DAUGHTER OF THOMAS BONNER
> OF CALLERTON WHO DIED OCT 7TH 1799 AGED 33
> ALSO OF THEIR SON JOHN WHO DIED AN INFANT"

The lettering is in the same style and probably the same hand as that on the west side of the Cross. The words give only the facts. There are no words of commendation or consolation.

The stone itself is the abdication of all art. When she looked at Michelangelo's Last Judgment in the Sistine Chapel, Sarah spoke of the inadequacy of human art to "even conceive the things of a future existence". Her response on her parents' grave is to produce a work that is all the more powerful because of its acceptance of the inability to say anything.

The beautiful Cross may cast its shadow on this stone of a summer evening, but this unsculpted stone with its simple lettering is the more eloquent memorial. The Cross recalls the faith of the Anglo-Saxons. The stone recalls time

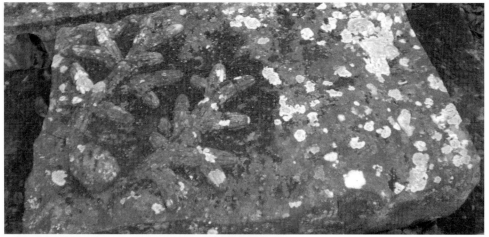

Above: the grave of Joseph Losh.
Left: the grave of Jane C. Losh.
Below: the grave of Margaret Losh and a detail of the pine cone and butterfly.

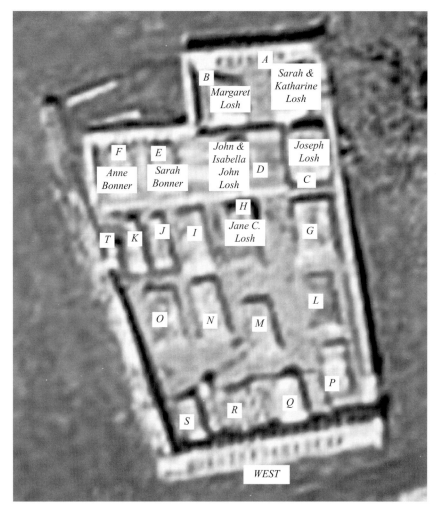

The Losh Burial Plot

A Katharine Isabella Losh died February 1835
Sarah Losh died 29th March 1853

B Margaret Losh died 29th December 1845

C Joseph Losh died 31st March 1848

D John Losh died 3rd March 1814
Isabella his wife died 7th October 1799
also of their son John who died an infant

E Sarah Bonner died 1st March 1840

F Anne Bonner died August 1846

G Colonel Losh died 12th March 1865

H Jane C. Losh died 29th October 1847

I Mary Kemmis died 31st December 1876

J Sara Spencer Losh died January 1883

K William Septimus Losh died Sept 1888

L Robert Henry Losh died 7th November 1867

M Alicia Margaret Losh 20th March 1872

N Elizabeth Evans 22nd July 1867

O Hannah Shepherd died 17th July 1861

P Henry Blakeney died 10th August 1884
Louisa Blakeney died 1st December 1872

Q Francis C Hutchinson died 6th October 1863

R Frances Hutchinson died 22nd November 1878

S Alice Margaret Adelaide Evans died 6th October 1856

T Stone in Memory of William Thain

90

Sarah Bonner's grave.

immemorial.

John Losh died in 1814 and was buried in Wreay Churchyard, but the gravestone might not have been made at that time. The infant John's burial was registered at St. Cuthbert's in Carlisle.

Joseph Losh's grave lies next to that of his parents. He had a severe mental impairment, and, as a result of John Losh's will, he was to be cared for by William Gaskin. He died on 21st Jan, 1848, and Sarah will have been responsible for the simple stone. Again the stone is unshaped. The inscription, now illegible, is confined to a corner and there is a motif of a fossil, (a clubmoss or crinoid) or of a cone or scallop shape out of which grow segmented branches.

Margaret, John Losh's sister, died on 29th December, 1845, and was buried at Wreay on 1st January, 1846. The unmarried Margaret had been mother and friend to Sarah and Katharine after their mother's death. The inscription on the grave reads:

"HERE LYE THE MORTAL REMAINS OF MARGARET LOSH WHO DIED DEC 29TH 1845. IN THE GLOOMY DAY OF TROUBLE SHE KEPT STEADFAST IN THE PATIENCE OF THAT HOPE WHICH FAILETH NOT & IN THE DARK HOUSE OF MORTAL DISSOLUTION THE PEACE OF THAT HOPE DEPARTED NOT FROM HER".

The words, redolent with the evangelical language of the time, may or may not have been Sarah's own. Margaret had poor health and there is a hint in James Losh's Diaries that she suffered from depression.

Again the motif akin to the 2cone and branches" is used, but here the motif is more definitely that of a pine cone and pine branches and there is a butterfly alighting on one branch. The use of this motif on the grave establishes the symbolic use Sarah Losh was making of both the cone and the butterfly.

The same style of motif is to be found on the gravestone of Jane C. Losh, who died in 1847. Here the motif is a tangle of branches bearing a small bird singing.

Sarah Losh may have been responsible for the graves of Sarah and Anne Bonner. This pair of gravestones is a more conventional copy of a templar or crusader style tomb. There are similar ones in Bridekirk near Cockermouth.

The motif on the grave of Colonel John Joseph Losh, who died after Sarah Losh, is similar to those on the other Losh family graves, but in this case it seems a pastiche of the originals: the Colonel, who served in India, lies in a grave beneath a palm tree with sheathed, crossed scimitars.

The gravestones reveal the sense of loss that must have been present to the Loshes in the 1840s. With George and his children having come to live in the area they constituted a small community. In the 1840s there were five deaths in the immediate family: Sarah Bonner on 1st March, 1840, and then four deaths in under three years: Margaret Losh on 29th December, 1845; Anne Bonner in August, 1846; Jane C. Losh on 29th October, 1847, and Joseph Losh on 31st March, 1848.

The other graves in the plot are those of members of the family who died after the death of Sarah Losh, except for the grave of Hannah Shepherd, who was a servant to both Sarah and Alicia Losh.

The mausoleum is described as druidic, cyclopean, archaic, Archaean, etc. It seems a transference of a weight of grief into stone. The walls are constructed of heavy, unshaped stone, apparently without mortar. The roof is made of heavy flags. The structure could not be simpler: four solid walls with two narrow window holes and a door. Around the top is a pediment. The copper door opens to reveal a wooden door cut crudely from the roughest wood that has now greyed with age. Inside the roof has needed the support of rude pillars which hold up an enormous weight of beams cut from red sandstone. The weight and the darkness are deeply oppressive.

In the shade of the stone chamber is a white marble statue whose beauty lightens the darkness. If you look through either window - you have to stand on tip-toe - you can glimpse the quiet profile of Katharine Losh gazing steadfastly downwards at a pine cone held in her lap. It is an image of complete serenity. The white contemplative stillness seems to breathe an assurance of a life to come.

The marble statue was carved by David Dunbar (1782 -1866), a pupil of Francis Chantrey, who had been instrumental in the founding of the Carlisle Academy. By the 1840s he had acquired a national reputation. Sarah commissioned him to copy a sketch she had made of Katharine sitting on the beach at Naples in 1817. The statue is dated 1850, but the Mausoleum is referred to in a Directory of 1847.

In three of the corners, quietly reposing in the shade and unseen from the

Above: the Mausoleum viewed from the north-east.
Below: the inner wooden door and the interior.

93

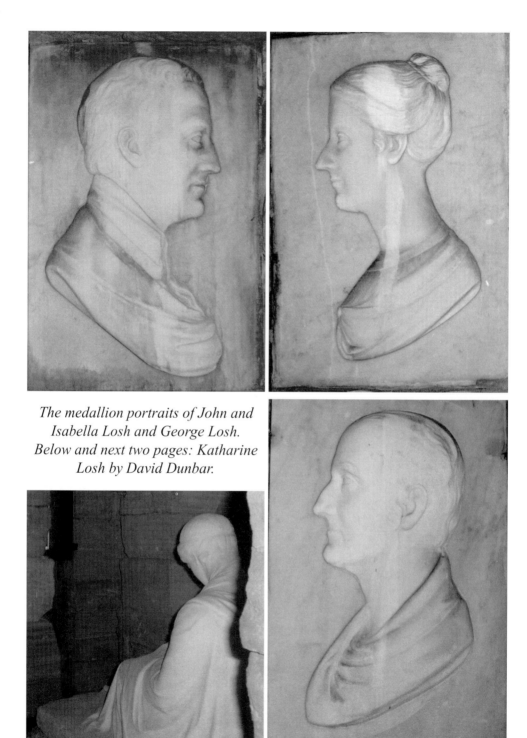

The medallion portraits of John and Isabella Losh and George Losh. Below and next two pages: Katharine Losh by David Dunbar.

outside, are marble reliefs of John, Isabella and George Losh. The fourth corner remains unoccupied.

The statue of Katharine has suffered over the years from water coming through the roof. The end of the nose has been damaged. A metal canopy has been fitted above the statue and metal mesh across the windows. The copper door, like the copper doors on the windows, is an unfortunate later addition,

Over the years Sarah Losh had a concern with wells. She re-used the belfry from the old church as the head of a well or trough for horses some fifty yards or so from the church on the Southwaite Road. About a mile along that road is Katharine's Well. It bears the date of 1867, but was almost certainly built by Sarah Losh at an earlier date. It is a larger structure than the other wells and it is topped by her characteristic arcade of small arches.

She also restored St. Ninian's Well at Brisco, setting a stone arch decorated with a diamond motif in the retaining wall. The well was supposed to be an ancient site associated with the saint, and it may have supplied water to Carlisle in Roman or Anglo-Saxon times. Sarah's interest in wells may have been associated with her interest in the early church. It may also have been motivated by her concern for animals. The last words of her will are: "I desire the old poney may be taken care of as at present & the old carriage horse also".

There seems to be little else to mark the last ten years or so of Sarah Losh's life. Hall talks of a folk memory of her walking, black-bonnetted, from Woodside to the Church. She gave money to schools in Wreay, Upperby and Hesket.

The books selected by Manchester College indicate that she continued to pursue her wide intellectual interests. One surprise among the titles is William Palmer's standard work on "The English Liturgy", which was originally published in 1836, but the volume from the Losh estate was the fourth edition, published in 1845, three years after she had so placed a stone communion table that the priest faced the congregation. Her wide interest in religion continued. She may have bought Alban Butler's twelve volume edition of "The Lives of the Saints", published in the 1840s and destined to become a very popular work; and five volumes of Cardinal Newman's works, from 1844/45 were found in the Woodside library. She was alive to the great religious controversies of the day and it is possible, if the very limited trace we have of her reading is any guide, that she was drawn towards Anglo-catholicism.

There were also several works on history: Joinville's "Chronicles of the Crusades" and Ockley's "History of the Saracens" both 1848; Brand's "Popular Antiquities of Great Britain" ,1849, and Collingwood Bruce on "The Roman Wall" ,1851. Among literary works, perhaps inevitably, there was a first edition of

Above: Katharine's Well.
Left: St Ninian's Well, Brisco.
Below: the Bell Well near the church.

98

Sarah Losh's signature as it appears on her will.

William Wordsworth's "Prelude" published in 1850, but there was also Schiller's "Das Lied von der Glocke" and that curious Elizabethan tome by Robert Burton, "The Anatomy of Melancholy".

Sarah Losh died on 29th March, 1853. She had been troubled by a bronchial complaint and was buried in the family plot in Wreay churchyard. The death certificate states the cause of death as "dysentery".

Her will was mistakenly dated the fourth day of September, 1851, instead of 1852. In this will she left the Woodside estate to her cousin, James Losh, the eldest son of her Uncle James. He had become head of the Losh family, since the line through John Losh was without issue, and he was, therefore, the principle beneficiary.

The will shows a concern to maintain a number of her cousins, mostly the daughters of George Losh, who had come to live in the vicinity and may have been dependent upon her. Her cousins, William Septimus Losh and his wife, Sarah, George's daughter, were left the property at Wreay Syke. She had purchased this property many years earlier in conjunction with Katharine. Similarly, the property at Ravenside was left to another cousin, Margaret Alicia Losh, another of George Losh's daughters, who remained unmarried and also received an annuity of £100 and the considerable sum of £3000. Sarah may have contributed to the design of both properties.

George's third daughter, Frances, who had married Francis Hutchinson, a doctor from the Isle of Man, and had lived in The Cottage at Brisco, was left the cottage and an annuity of fifty pounds and a lump sum of £2000. A further sum of £2500 was left to another cousin, John Warwick, her mother's nephew with the specific purpose of paying off the debt on Birtley Hall near Chester-le Street, in County Durham.

A hundred pounds was left to the children of William Gaskin. Small sums of money were left to local people including ten pounds to Hannah Shepherd, who is the only person not belonging to the Losh family to be buried in the Losh Burial Enclosure. Hannah was also left a mahogany chest of drawers and Sarah Losh's clothes. Small sums were left for mourning costumes for the servants at Woodside and there were small donations to charities as well: "I leave to the blind orphans at Newcastle the school at Upperby & dispensary at Carlisle £20 each".

In the codicil, which had originally been attached to an earlier will, and was dated nine months earlier on 23rd December, 1851, she leaves small sums to her cousins' husbands and other people. There are a number of articles which she singles out such as: Roman mosaics to be made into "broaches" for Miss Kemmis and Miss Cussans; a copy of William Billings's account of Carlisle Cathedral for William Septimus Losh; and an oil sketch of Tynemouth that was "now in the south entrance" for Mr Townly.

The will concerned itself with the distribution of an extremely valuable estate. But Sarah Losh was also interested in ensuring that small sums of money were given to a wide number of individuals and there was a very particular care that various articles went to the appropriate person.

Sarah Losh was a very wealthy woman when she died. She chose to a have the simplest of funerals and Lonsdale stresses that the obituary in the local paper was the briefest possible.

In concluding her will she stipulates that five pounds should be given "to the Wreay poor at my funeral which must be as private & inexpensive as possible".

The stone that covers the graves of Sarah and Katharine carries the inscription:

> "KATHARINE ISABELLA LOSH,
> DIED FEBRUARY, 1835, AGED 47.
> SARAH LOSH,
> DIED MARCH 29TH, 1853.
> IN VITA DIVISAE, IN MORTE CONJUNCTAE.
> LORD LET THY MERCY LIGHTEN UPON US."

Katharine's name is in smaller letters. "In vita divisae, in morte conjunctae." (In life divided, in death united.) The elegant, disciplined Latin parallelism hides and reveals a depth of feeling. The selection of the verse: "Lord let thy mercy lighten upon us," suggests a prepossessing sense of the weight that lies upon the dead and a belief in God's mercy. The word "lighten" carries two of the central metaphors in Sarah Losh's work: they are to be seen in the mass of stone that weighs down on the Mausoleum and the fragile beam of light that shines on Katharine.

The gravestone is divided unevenly into three sections by two parallel diagonal cuts. In the central panel, which has a flat surface, is the inscription in the simplest of lettering, as though cut by an unskilled hand. It is the same lettering as that on the Cross. The upper triangle is just the uncut stone. The lowest section

has been carved but so crudely that the motif appears as though it were part of the stone itself. Two ugly, bulbous cones, or possibly shells, or a fossil clubmoss, are the source of a small tightly branched, lined and segmented growth. It seems neither plant nor fossil but it appears as though life might emerge out of the fabric of the very stone. Lonsdale says that it is "a large coralline and scallop-shell, which the good lady herself used to associate with the pilgrimage through life".

The edges of the stones are now covered with the encroachments of ground ivy, and loose earth and dust and lichen hide the bare rock.

Sarah Losh had raised powerful images to the beauty of life out of the depth of her grief, but her final monument is the simplest and most powerful poetic statement of all.

A Photographic Survey of St. Mary's Church, Wreay.

Above: the west end. Below: the north side.

Above: the south side.   Below: the apse and the east end

The west door and the arch surround.

*The fossil window with its carvings of cones, ammonites and other fossils: a ceratites,
a crinoid, a staghorn coral and a nudibranch mollusc and two flower-like forms.*

The middle window with its carvings of poppies, butterflies, chrysalis, lilies and wheat.

The right hand window with its carvings of cones, a bird, an owl, a cockchafer,
a bee (?), and possibly fir branches bearing cones.

Part of the arcade of windows in the west end with the statues of St. Peter and Paul.
The sundial and the eagle.

The "crocodile" and the "snake" on the south side.

The "gargoyles" on the north side; The "winged turtle" and (below) the "tortoise" and the "dragon" that served as a chimney.

The door, interior, with its beautifully carved surround and the cone handles.

Details of the door frame showing two butterflies on a gourd carved by Robert Donald, the gardener at Woodside.

Above: the cone handles on the inside of the door.
Below left: one of the dripstone cones by the west door.
Below right: one of the cone pillars by the steps down from the baptistry.

The roof timbers with the pendant cones marking the line of the nave.

The north window in the west wall.

Above: the south and middle windows in the west end.
Below: two of the windows in the nave.

116

Two of the sets of clerestory windows from the north and south sides. The left and right windows are made of glass fragments, the centre probably of alabaster.

Above: The apse. Below, left: a lotus candlestick.
Right: One of the eagles supporting the communion table.

The communion table made of Italian marble with bronze supports in the form of eagles. Above: viewed from the east. Below: from the west.

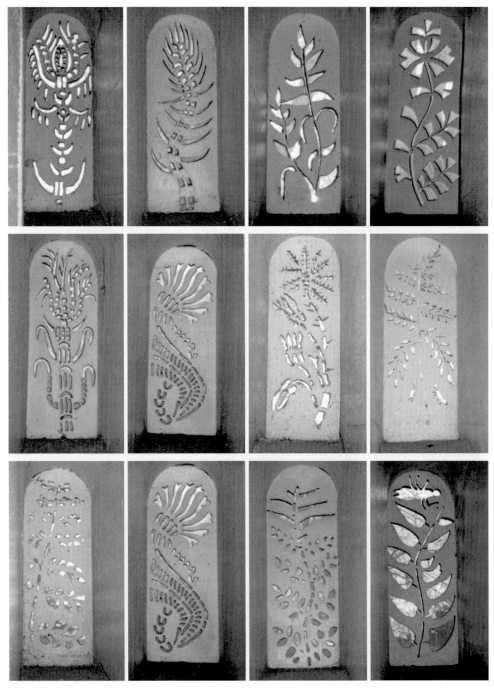

Twelve of the thirteen clerestory windows in the apse made from alabaster cutouts, displaying various plant and fossil forms.

A section of the painted wall that runs around the apse.

"Ecce Agnus Dei" - the image at the centre of the apse and opposite
the emblems of six of the apostles.

The bird on the capital of the south-west column and the bat and bird with a lizard on the north-west column in the apse.

Ten of the capitals in the apse carved with patterned images of flowers, leaves and ferns.

The head of a young woman on the south of the chancel arch.
Inset: detail of Dunbar's statue of Katharine in the Mausoleum.

The head of the bearded man that projects from the north side of the chancel arch.

The nave and chancel showing the furnishings. A - the shelf with seven angels and eight palm trees. B - the archangel on the bat pedestal. C - the archangel on the dragon pedestal.
D - the cock and owl bracket.(see left) E - the eagle lectern. F - the pelican lectern.
G - the pulpit and palm candle-holder.

The archangel holding a lily, on the left of the chancel arch. On the pedestal is an image of a bat chasing a butterfly.

129

The archangel to the right of the chancel arch.

The pulpit made from bog oak, with the calamites (horsetails) candle-holder.

The stork lectern .

The eagle lectern.

Above:The font showing the dove and the grape-vine.
Below: The font showing the melon.

Above: The font showing the water lily and the lotus flower.
Below: The font showing the butterfly, wheat and the dragonfly.

Above:The font showing the melon, pomegranate and pine or, perhaps, fern sora.
Below:The silvered top of the font with its alabaster waterlilies and lotus flowers.

Henry Lonsdale and Sarah Losh

Henry Lonsdale was born in Carlisle on 25th February, 1816, when Sarah Losh was thirty years old. His father was a tradesman. At fifteen he was apprenticed to the leading medical practice in the city and then, three years later, went to Edinburgh to study medicine.

After graduating in 1838, suffering from overwork, he retired to the comparative quiet of a country practice at Raughton Head, within a few miles of Woodside. He was very active in the area: he was a founding member of the Inglewood Agricultural Society, gave scientific lectures and was a keen advocate of the Cumberland Muse, Susanna Blamire. Susanna Blamire was an unpublished eighteenth century poet who had lived in nearby Stockdalewath and had written a very able long poem of country life named after the village, as well as attractive lyrics in both dialect and standard English. Lonsdale later published her work. The Blamire family belonged to the rural gentry and moved in the same circles as the Loshes, Jane Blamire being her intimate friend. It is possible that Lonsdale came to know Sarah Losh at this time, although he remained in the area for under two years. It is almost certain that he was never acquainted with Katharine.

He returned to Edinburgh where he had a brief, busy and distinguished career, before he again retreated to Carlisle. This time he was suffering from bronchial problems.

In 1846 he was appointed physician to the Cumberland Infirmary and from then on he became closely involved in the public health of the city.

It is at this time he probably came to be better acquainted with Sarah Losh. He established a sanitary association in Carlisle and was publishing medical papers which received national attention. His wide culture, interests and radical politics would have recommended him. He implies, in his biographical note, in passing, that he was a dinner guest at Woodside. He also claims to be a close friend. In the anecdote about the reading of Baron von Reichenbach, he smoothly indicates how he was readily admitted to the retiring lady's spartan private rooms: "Only special friends were admitted to this sanctum in the upper storey, where I found her one morning in a laughing humour from reading Baron von Reichenbach's "Researches on the Dynamics of Magnetism, Electricity, &c., in their relation to Vital Force ". He also, equally smoothly, mentions his "friend, George Eliot". Sarah Losh was 59 when Lonsdale, then 29, returned to Carlisle in 1845, and she had eight more years to live.

Lonsdale married Eliza Indiana Bond in 1851 and seems to have settled into the life of a gentleman, living in a fine house, Rose Hill, two miles east of Carlisle, and travelling widely on the continent. He became an enthusiast for continental, and especially Italian, art and architecture. He retained his post at the Cumberland Infirmary until 1868, but his later years were devoted to the writing of biographies on notable locals, including Doctor Heysham and the sculptor, Musgrave Lewthwaite Watson. The six volumes of "The Cumberland Worthies", which contains the account of Sarah Losh together with brief notices of her father and uncles, began publication in 1867.

Lonsdale was writing at least fifteen years after Sarah Losh's death. He indicates that he had access to private papers. He was able to read what must have been an exceptional journal of her continental tour and her personal notes on history and possibly much else in the personal papers of a highly articulate woman, but nothing of her poetry and other literary writing. He probably had the full support of the surviving family and certainly would have been in close contact for many years with many people who knew her well. He claims a close acquaintance with Miss Losh and was well qualified temperamentally and intellectually to be her biographer. He certainly admired her, and, for someone thirty years her junior, seems very smitten by her physical appearance.

However, there is always the question of the extent to which we are being presented with a very determinedly Henry Lonsdale's "Sara Losh". The issue is most pertinent in relation to the interpretation of the church where it is difficult to discern which ideas have been derived from Sarah Losh and which are the product of Lonsdale's own well-informed understanding or the views of his fellow doctor and mythographer friend, Thomas Inman.

Despite these quibbles, it goes without saying that we are fortunate to have such an able, if brief, biography of Sarah Losh by a near contemporary.

SARA LOSH

"Quiete et pure atque eleganter acta aetatis placida et lenis recordatio."-Cicero.

In the obituary of the Carlisle newspapers of April 1853 is the following: "At Woodside, near Carlisle, on the 29th ult., Miss Losh."

Such a record - and no simpler one could have been made of the death of any of her Majesty's subjects, high or low - caused surprise, if not a little mortification, among the friends of the deceased lady, who had hoped to see an appropriate tribute to the memory of a gentlewoman of such exemplary worth and benevolence. The brevity of the announcement implied such consonance with the sentiments of one who sought to be veiled from newspaper comment, that I had no hesitation in attributing its dictation to the departed one herself. The general public, however, cognisant of the high repute of Miss Losh, could not fail to note the contrast of less than a line of print being bestowed on a lady of inestimable excellence, whilst not unfrequently columns of panegyric are lavished on a lucky coster-monger and babbling political partisan.

> " Strongest minds
> Are often those of whom the noisy world
> Hears least, else surely this lady had not left
> Her graces unrevealed and unproclaimed."[1]

Whilst mindful of the cherished retirement of my much lamented friend, and freely admitting the difficulty of portraying the rare endowments of both her mind and person, I

[1] *See editorial Notes pages 162-3*

Above: Sarah Losh as she appears in the portrait accompanying Lonsdale's memoir.

am led to believe that this series of Cumberland Worthies would be looked upon as incomplete without the name of Sara Losh of Woodside. As an excuse for my effort I may plead, in the spirit of the words quoted above from Cicero: "Placid and soothing is the remembrance of a life passed in quietness, innocence, and elegance," and hope to trace, in outlined form, a life marked by high intellectual claims, a large philanthropy, exquisite taste and refinement, conjoined with a rare amiability and loveliness of person.

Sara* Losh, the subject of this memoir, was the oldest daughter of John and Isabella Losh of Woodside, and probably born on or about New Year's Day 1786. She was baptized at St Cuthbert's, Carlisle, by the Rev. Dr. Carlyle, on January 6, 1786. Her sister, Katharine Isabella, was baptized in the same church on February 11, 1788.

From infantile life Sara Losh showed the esprit of her sex; she was lively, talkative, and intelligent, and not without some petulancy of temper, arising from undue sensitiveness to any interference with her own wishes. This shadow, the only cloud on her brow, it was needful to dispel; and it is worthy of note, as instancing her fortitude, that she mastered the impetuous feeling, the only enemy that stood in the way of a perfect amiability.

The two sisters Losh had the benefit of a first-class education, at home, in Bath, and in London. Sara made great progress in Italian and French, Latin and Greek, music and mathematics, indeed trespassed rather closely upon the heels of her teachers, one of whom regarded her as a classic scholar of incomparable excellence for her age and sex.

Upon the death of Mrs Losh in 1799, the household management of Woodside fell to the care of Miss Margaret Losh, who also acted as guide and counsellor to her nieces. Though so many years have passed away since my introduction to "Aunt Margaret" Losh, her presence is still fresh in my memory. She was then advanced in years and time had not wholly spared the finer lineaments of form and face; yet through the ivory complection of her visage the elemental structure of classical elegance was visible; whilst she retained a brightness and touching beauty of her own. Her high-worn black dress, her waist bound by a rope-like belt, to which her keys were hanging and not less her general costume and demeanour, befitted a lady abbess. Her calm, courteous dignity, the charming affability of her conversation, in which refined sentiment and worldly experience happily blended, impressed strangers as typifying the grace and culture of the true English gentlewoman. She was extolled at home, and in her companionship of her nieces, claimed no small regard from strangers beyond the Alps. Italians of aesthetic feeling saw in her symmetry and face their beau ideal of the daughters of ancient Rome; and the Cavaliere Lande, president of the academy at Rome, then engaged on the subject of Coriolanus, and unable to find a proper model to finish Valeria, sought the good offices of Signor Caputi to persuade Miss Margaret

*Up to her thirtieth year, if not much later in life, Miss Losh spelt her name Sara, as she liked it better than Sarah, which she used in her more mature years. For her autograph Sara Losh has been adopted, and will be used in this memoir. The baptismal register is not so good a guide as many would suppose; thus Mrs. Losh's name is registered "Elizabeth" as the mother of Sara, but "Isabella" as the mother of Katherine Isabella!

Losh to sit for the character, to which application, however, she did not accede. If the Roman ladies, fifty years ago, impaired their expression in extreme embonpointe, as Sara Losh thought, so as to become imperfect representatives of the heroic blood of their ancestors, the art treasures of the Capitol and Vatican should surely have afforded types for the artist seeking to commemorate the historical Coriolanus, amid his feminine relations - a noble group, of a noble age, rendered so aptly and grandly in the pages of Shakespeare.

At the dawn of this century, numbers of families repaired to Carlisle for the winter months; some to avoid the inclement exposure of their rural mansions; others sought the city for its liveliness and society. And for young people there was no want of attractions - the Cathedral and Canons expectant; the garrison and its gay Lotharios; the Carlisle Hunt of squires and ladies fair, all dressed in white and green; the dances of the "upper ten", and the public assemblies, to which latter the young ladies of Woodside had to be introduced. No wonder that the county families blessed with budding daughters left their solitary mansions, leafless trees, and brown fallows, for the Border city, its pretty environs, its urban life, and gladsome associations.

Most elegantly attired, and no less elegant in person and carriage, Miss Losh created a sensation in the Coffee-house ballroom. Being little heard of outside her family circle, her presentation not only partook of the freshness due to sweet seventeen, but was greatly enhanced by personal features declared to be perfect, and a marked refinement that bespoke educated intelligence. She was at once assigned the place of belle, and since the days of Sara Blamire, no one remembered so great a beauty. Her admiring aunts, both exceedingly pretty women, looked upon her as "an angel visiting the ballroom to mingle with poor human creatures." Many years subsequently, when Miss Losh took her seat in the French opera at Paris, all eyes were turned to the "English beauty," and from various parts of the theatre were heard, "Quelle belle femme!" "Charmante!" &c.

Though educated far beyond the reach of her own sex, and, indeed, of most men, she had no idea of resting upon the scholastic training of her earlier years. Under the worthy Parson Gaskin*[2] of Wreay she kept up her Latin and Greek, but looked mainly to herself for modern languages. In art she took special interest; in science and the higher culture she occasionally passed an hour. Whilst feminine pursuits were in the foreground of her thoughts,

*The Rev. William Gaskin of Wreay was an able classic and mathematician, who lived on intimate terms with the Loshes, indeed so highly did he esteem the family, that though a poor incumbent, he refused the offer of a valuable living of the Earl of Egremont's rather than part from them. Previous to holding the incumbency of Wreay, he used to do clerical duty at High Head and Sebergham, and in returning to Woodside from these places, rode over the unenclosed ground of Broadfield, finding his way at night as best he could along the horse-track wild, amid swampy surfaces, showing abundant phosphorescent light, the tramping through which disconcerted his steed, yet mightily interested himself. He belonged to the old school of country parsons who could enjoy a fox-hunt and cock-fight as well as his Greek Testament. In his day Latin quotations were not unfrequently part of the symposial conversation, and if any false quantities or misquotations were heard, Gaskin caught them, and at once put the defaulter right, be he Chancellor or Dean! Miss Losh being pretty alert in the same direction, rejoiced to see her old teacher airing his erudite and classic lore. Gaskin

nothing came amiss that was likely to contribute to her mental improvement.

In study, in drawing and embroidery, pleasant in their variety and in their aims, in the cultivation of flowers and the beautifying of her residence, Sara Losh filled up her time, and seldom retired before midnight. Drowsy inertness and the ennui that is but the reflex of sloth and imbecility, and both incompatible with healthy feminine nature, obtained no place with the loving sisters, who, in the midst of their home occupations, found both time and opportunity to promote good and charitable works. I call them loving sisters, but words will never convey their deep and affectionate attachment. They were ever together in unison of thought, in action and purpose; yet they were of a different temperament: Sara was quiet, humorous, and intellectual; Katharine was hearty and vivacious, and radiant as sunshine itself.

Woodside possessed happy advantages in its social life, its intellectual gatherings, and pleasant amenities. Within good neighbourhood was Dr William Paley[3], the moral and political philosopher, who could elucidate natural-history forms with a morphological instinct, and be no less a preacher and propounder of the evidences of his faith. At Woodside, Paley was *en accord* with mine host, enjoyed his joke and bit of pleasantry, and never failed as a trencher-man. Then there were the eminent Laws, father and sons, all bishops in their time, Dean Milner[4], the Rev. Dr Carlyle[5], Sir Joseph Gilpin[6], Dr Heysham[7]; and among distant visitors, the Earl of Dundonald[8], and John (afterwards Sir John) Leslie[9]* of Edinburgh, of European fame as a physicist, - all men of note in their respective walks, who laboured to extend the boundaries of human knowledge in the direction of history, statistics, divinity, and philosophy. Mingling with these superior men under the Losh roof-tree were the Blamire family of the Oaks[10], the Warwicks of Warwick Hall[11], the Grahams of Low House[12], and the leading gentry.

Society of this character was sure to influence the impressionable nature of Sara Losh, whose mental discipline had been the most prominent feature of her life. Indeed one of her London masters was so struck with her capacity that he offered her various subjects of study,

was oft the guest of his Bishop and Dean Milner; and many a tussle the latter and he had on matters scholarly and controversial; but the parson complained of the late hours of the Abbey, and of his inability to contend with the learned Dean at two o'clock in the morning, inasmuch as his brandy potations were not so potent in argument as the Dean's opium-taking! What led Dr Milner to opium is a mystery, but he must have been as early in the field as Coleridge, and De Quincey, the great confessor. The Rev. Mr Gaskin died in 1832, at the age of eighty or more years, and was much regretted.

*The company of such men as Leslie at Woodside implies that John Losh took interest in subjects seldom entered upon by country squires. Leslie unbent himself at Woodside by wearing a somewhat curious garb, and collecting snails and insects, all which were so foreign to the bucolic mind that he was viewed as "an oddity." His experiments within doors, and ready communicativeness to please the young ladies at Woodside, may have given Sara a taste for philosophic reading, that found further interest in the Chemical Works of Walker, in which her father was so deeply interested.

*In 1852 I introduced Father Gavazzi to Miss Losh, who conversed with him in French, then in Italian, so as to adapt herself to what she considered his wishes. The Padre was so charmed by her conversation that on my incidentally meeting him in 1863, on the banks of the Arno, his first inquiry was after the lady of Woodside, whom he had seen but once, and that was eleven years previously.

and the higher he aimed the higher she soared. With powers to grapple with Euclid and algebra, she had but to give her attention to any subject to master it. Reading aloud to the home circle was a great pastime of the Losh family, and the winter evenings at Woodside were oft the pleasantest part of the diurnal. Fond of classics, Sara would read a Latin author off-hand, and in so quiet a style as to lead to no suspicion of its being the translation of the moment. One evening, after an effort of this kind, she was called out of the room; and a visitor, one of the listening party, wishing to he informed on some message, took up the book and discovered the Latinity without a line of English, much to his surprise, if not incredulity. She was well read in Greek, and studied it three hours daily, till she could render any Greek play almost at sight. She spoke French and Italian fluently. Of German and Spanish she knew very much less. Logical and comprehensive in thought, her reading embraced, *inter alia,* political economy, the more recondite histories, and not a few works pertaining to philosophy itself.

Miss Losh was slightly above the middle stature of women, elegant in figure and graceful throughout. She had a full frontal development, and adorning a perfect female head were brown tresses of luxuriant growth sufficient to hide the innocence of a Naiad in her sylvan sportings, or to be adapted to any style of fashion; a beautiful complexion; blue eyes, with a shade of grey; dark eyebrows; a fine Roman nose, and no less fine bust. No art production could satisfactorily render the grouped loveliness of a face like Miss Losh's when under the spell of the finer emotions. Neither the miniature of Carrick[13], taken in her fiftieth year, upon which the accompanying portrait is based, nor the bust sculptured by D. Dunbar, both local artists, convey a true portraiture. Nothing less than Greek art, the sculpturesque, could have done justice to her features and intellectual cast, or, as it may be termed, that singularly classical air in her physiognomy. Classical in mould, she was no less classical in thought and culture. You looked upon Miss Losh's face in her latter days as one in which character rather than feature was the attraction. In dress she conformed to female fashion, and dressed gaily and expensively; but with advancing years she had a greater regard for comfort and suitability. The death of her only sister in 1835, to whom she was so devotedly attached, led to the adoption of sombre colours as external emblems of a truly perpetual mourning. A black bonnet of cottage shape, a gown of artless make and merino texture, with shawl to match, constituted her garb out of doors, showing a subdued drapery of external forms befitting her retirement from the more busy world.

Whilst elegance ruled the reception-rooms of Woodside, her own apartment showed polished boards, a deal table for her book and needle-work, a basket of cloven wood for the fire-dogs (andiron), and upon the plastered walls a few engravings. Only special friends were admitted to this sanctum in the upper storey, where I found her one morning in a laughing humour from reading Baron von Reichenbach's "Researches on the Dynamics of Magnetism, Electricity, &c., in their relation to Vital Force"[15] - a highly theoretic work pertaining to physiology and psychology, if not divination, that did not comport with the fine

143

logical acumen of Miss Losh. The circumstance is mentioned here to illustrate the character of her reading and the readiness with which she could detect pseudo-science from that based on legitimate deductions.

She relished a really good book of the thoughtful, suggestive, and historical stamp, and was not slow to appreciate the capital novels of Scott[16], Lytton[17], the Ostade pictures of Dickens[18], and the satirical hits at modern society by Thackeray[19]. Archaeology had many and lasting attractions to her, not only as a study *per se*, illustrating the curiosities of ancient and medieval structures, but as, viewed with an historic or architectural meaning, realising to modern eyes the life of the past. Having a library rich in every department of literature, she kept herself *au courant* with passing events and the history of the times - its politics, its social progress and improving arts. She saw *in prospectu*, and oft spoke of, the benefits likely to accrue from more diffused information upon the habits and comforts of the people.

Miss Losh was fertile in thought, and found gratification in filling pages of manuscript with both prose and verse. Unfortunately she preserved nothing but the journal or diary she kept of her Continental tours. This record of her travels, made from day to day, embraced her experience of several months in France, Germany, Italy, Switzerland, &c., in company with her sister, and her uncle, William Losh. As good works of travels were scarce fifty years ago, it is much to be regretted that a book rendered from a woman's point of view, and guided by intellectuality and good taste, was not made known to the public. In every page of her seven manuscript copy-books there is to be found readable and interesting matter, descriptive scenes, architectural notices; and observations on men and manners: and all so full of freshness and point. The chief excellence of the journal is to be found in her criticism of the pictures and sculpture and other works of art in the grand galleries of Italy.

In a few words of preface to her journal, the object of which was merely to preserve, as she writes, "my recollections unaltered, not to eke them out with information which other travellers might furnish. Such information I may be glad to meet with, but have no wish to copy nor right to pilfer." If she had made any "erroneous assertions," she hoped the blame might rest with the "*ciceroni*", those blind guides of the blind, of whom half reply in the words which the proverb assigns to blockheads "I do not know;" while the other half conceal their ignorance by means of their invention." The journal displays a lively knowledge of ancient and modern history, archaeology, and the fine arts in general, interspersed with classical quotations from Latin, Greek, and Italian authors, showing by their aptness a thorough familiarity with the authors, from Homer and Catullus down to Dante and Petrarch.

A few extracts will convey her style. Here is a description of the picturesque town of Pont l'Echelle[20] on the eve of, and on Rogation Sunday[21] 1817:-

"We were soon surrounded by poor people, who begged with great vociferation. Some of the women had goitres, which did not, however, induce them to lay aside their gold necklaces. The children were in general pretty, but the most persevering beggars we had ever met with, as they followed us for miles, after our stock of small money was exhausted, with a clamour which one felt almost heartless to listen to. The 'Croix Blanche,' at which we had taken up our quarters, was an inn of a very primitive appearance, and promised little accommodation, we found, however, clean linen, silver forks, and good potatoes, now in general estimation.

"Tuesday, 29th, We were awakened by the singing of psalms in the street - a sound which we concluded indicative of a funeral, but learnt that it was a Rogation-Day procession; and were further informed by the old hostess, with some satisfaction, that her husband walked at the head of the men, and her daughter at the head of the women. We hurried out to gain a sight of the procession, than which one of greater simplicity could not be imagined, yet the effect was pleasing and impressive. It was early morn, the mists still rested on the hills, and the dew spread its pearly fretwork on the valley; all was still and solemn, not a breeze disturbed the blossoms, nor was a human creature to be seen stirring, except where, turning the point of a jutting crag, a long line of villagers, clothed simply in white, moved slowly forwards, sometimes chanting an artless hymn, sometimes kneeling devoutly to implore the divine blessing on their humble fields and returning labours. As the procession approached we observed more exactly the order of it. First came a number of the poorest persons, preceded by a banner and two lanterns, which were carried by men in white surplices; next were two rows of women, clothed in white linen, with muslin veils, some holding a prayer book, some a rosary. Then came the men in the same manner followed by the cure bearing aloft the crucifix, which was covered with a black scarf. On each side of him was carried a lantern. Though the primary object of these ceremonies is to obtain the fructification of the earth, yet those who partake in them, become linked in a sort of association to one another and contract or cement the obligation to reciprocal offices of kindness and charity. A remnant of such observances may still be traced in England amongst the gardeners, who on a particular day of the year go in regular order to church and hear a sermon. The grand and gloomy scenery of Savoy seems well calculated to heighten religious feelings. It was amongst scenes nearly similar, in the recesses of the mountains of Dauphiny, that St Bruno[22] fixed the spot of his mournful seclusion, the original Chartreuse, which we greatly regretted we could not take time to visit. In process of time the institution had become a rich one; and at the time of the Revolution had three hundred inmates, about twenty of whom had lately returned to the monastery. Twelve hours out of the twenty-four they spend in the church. They never make a repast in common, live almost wholly on potatoes, and, except on Thursdays, are never permitted to interchange a single word. Whether or no such a life might fit one for death, it would have the effect of reconciling one to it."

Miss Losh found a bookseller's wife in Chambery[23] complaining of a new tax imposed on paper, and citing the observation of Rousseau[24], who gave it as a proof of the preference of the inhabitants for eating to reading, that for one bookseller's shop there were twenty restaurants. She looked at the house where Rousseau visited Madame Warens[25], on the outside of which was a marble slab inscribed with some verses to the memory of "the eloquent, indignant, and querulous enthusiast," concluding with these lines:

145

" Il osa consacrer sa vie
A la gloire, et a la verite,
Et fut toujours persecute
Par lui-meme ou par 1'envie:[26]

At Spoleto[27] her attention was drawn to the hermitages on the wooded steeps, the retreats of French noblemen (during the sway of the Revolutionists) who wished to shade their invidious dignities under the garb of religion. The founder of this semi-religious community had returned to his estates and to reassert his consequence, and this circumstance leads Miss Losh to remark:-

"His selection of a place of retirement does honour to his taste; and his subsequent quitting it seems only to prove that every object of rational gratification-books, leisure, tranquillity, polished society, the luxuries of a city, the freedom of a desert, the influence of the softest climate and the most delightful scenery, are all insufficient to human enjoyment if devoid of the animation and contest, the charm of variety, the self-importance of activity, and, above all, the inspiring vanity of schemes and projects."

Though feeling the influence of the southern sun, she looked in vain for traces of its gentleness in the manners of the people; and her experience of Terracino was by no means favourable :

"We were attended both by dogs and cats during supper, which consisted of rice swimming in water, peas swimming in oil, and fish swimming in goat's milk, with cheese, apples, and fennel-root, to be washed down with wine literally impregnated with flies, as the bottles are seldom corked. On retiring for the night, we opened our windows to look at the prospect, and so mild was the air that we sat long listening to the sounds of the waves, which, shining like silver in the moonbeams, dashed with violence against the rocky shore.

"It was such a night as that which Virgil assigns to Aeneas when he sailed from this very shore where Caieta still gives her name to Gaita.

" Aspirant aura in noctem: nec candida cursum
Luna negat : splendet tremolo sub lumine pontes."[29]

A few words on Pompeii[30] may be quoted:

"We had been charmed successively with the view from the terrace of the villa of Diomides[31] and that which presented itself as we descended the steps of the platform on which stood the temple of Jupiter, looking over the Forum; but the view from the upper ranges of the amphitheatre exceeded in beauty, grandeur, and fascination all that we had ever seen or could have imagined. The superb structure on which one stands, the buried city which it touches, the luxuriant scenery of the coast beyond, the sea, the islands, and an amphitheatre of lofty mountains, in which the dark, ringed peak of Vesuvius contrasted with the deep blue tints of the other eminences, a bright sun, a transparent atmosphere, formed a combination the exquisite perfection of which no description and no painting can convey even a faint idea of. Yet in such a scene a refined audience could fix their attention on the brutal strife of the avenue, and turn from the soft loveliness of nature to watch the writhings of agonised conflict."

Her visit to Paestum[32] is so full of incident and excellent narrative that I regret much the brevity of my space:

"Of a scene more calculated than Paestum to inspire melancholy it is impossible to form an idea. At Pompeii we had seen the dwellings of ordinary mortals, as destroyed yet preserved, by a preternatural calamity; at Paestum, whence all meaner relics have disappeared, we seemed to tread the footsteps of superior beings, whose temples still remain to attest their preeminence; yet of this people, so elegant and so enlightened, no other trace is now in existence. By a long succession of the most common casualties they have vanished from the earth, and their place knoweth them no more. Of their history every record has perished. The name of Leucania[33] incites no recollections; and not one even of those, twice-flowering roses with which her luxurious sons were crowned now survive in the ruined Posidonia[33], to scatter fragrance over their profound sepulchres. Lizards crawl unheeded over the symbol of the Syren, which still is seen on the solitary gateway. The peasant only examines the wrecks of fallen magnificence lest he break his ploughshare against some prostrate capital; but the rude mariner, whose mind is more susceptible of impressions of splendour and magnitude, gazes with reverence on the elevated pillars, and wonders how the angels transported them from Palestine. The mind reverts with profoundest emotion to departed ages, and contrasts the state of these temples when filled with the votaries of a pompous worship, with what they present at this moment, when their silence is only disturbed by the plaints of a few squalid wretches, whose haggard faces even more than their patched attire excites the compassion of travellers. It seems as if Fate but spared a casual trophy of human art and of human glory to remind succeeding ages that the feebler works they produce will still more entirely and more speedily decay."

At Rome, writing of the studios and the taste shown for art, Miss Losh thus adverts to the formation of works for purchasers:

"The prevalent passion for descriptive poetry excites also fresh love for the landscape, and calls out the talents of numberless artists, while the loftier and severer studies of him who would embody action, and character arc not appreciated nor rewarded. Saints are contemned and angels disbelieved , and devils no longer wondered at. The ancient Greeks and Romans cause ennui, the Saracens are nearly forgotten, and modern hcroes are most unbecomingly dressed."

In describing the Sistine Chapel, she writes:

" It is a spacious and gloomy hall, one end of which is entirely covered with the famous fresco of the 'Last Judgment', considered the grandest and most terrific composition of the pencil, but the awful catastrophe it images seems little to weigh on the minds of the cardinals when assembled here to elect a pope. It is, after all, but painting, and the more wonderful it is, the more it convinces one that the utmost faculties of man are inadequate to portray or even conceive the things of a future existence. In this picture all is gloomy and horrible, yet sometimes even so ludicrous that one fancies Buonarotti insensible himself to the deep feelings he intended to excite, sporting with the fears and credulity of the people till his sport has the malice of the demons he exhibits. Correggio[35] was a stranger to the spirits of Paradise, but he painted forms fit to embody its messengers - bright, beneficent, and blissful; Michael Angelo has evoked fiends and conjured hell to appal mankind to aspire after heaven."

On the day following her visit to the Sistine Chapel, Signor Magrini read to the Losh party his dissertation on Michael Angelo's "Last Judgment," and seemed shocked at Miss Losh saying that the devils had the most satisfactory part in it.

A few extracts will show her opinion of Guido's "Aurora," one of the most celebrated frescoes (Palazzo Rospigliosi) in Rome:

"A second Prometheus appears to have stolen from the sun-beams the golden radiance that emanates from the car of Apollo. It is drawn by steeds whose hoofs spurn the liquid clouds, and which, hot, wild, and fiery, scarcely bear to he curbed by the God of Day, whose glowing visage, like that of an Olympic victor, is expressive of joy and impatience. The blooming hours which dance around the car are brilliant with the light reflected from it, and above it floats the star of morning under the emblem of a youthful geni with a torch. This admirable group is preceded by Aurora, who, skimming lightly on empurpled mists, flings on the earth gay flowers as she passes. Her visage is half shaded by a fleecy veil which partakes of the character of the dawn; her arms are most exquisitely formed, and a saffron drapery flows gracefully around her. Then the diminished landscape beneath is calm and peaceful, and strongly reminded us of the scenery near Ancona. It consists of a few simple objects - a dark blue sea with a few vessels in perfect repose; a distant mast in dim obscurity; and a foreground of dark brown, from whence the shades of night seem about to be chased. The contrast of the earth and air is as strong as possible, yet their harmony is that of nature itself; and such is the fascination of the whole, that one knows not how to relinquish the contemplation of it. The attention is riveted by the simple energy of the composition and the luminous tone that pervades it. All is powerful and all graceful; for the artist has felt and confided in his own lofty genius, and in the serene grandeur of the subject he has chosen. To fix the clouds and embody the sunrise is a task no mortal can perform; but in his image of this sublime spectacle he has seized on that which creates in the mind analogous sensations; and if not to the eye, at least to the fancy, has conveyed the impression of that beautiful scene which revives all nature, and kindles in the soul fresh life and ecstasy."

In another walk her pen had been actively engaged, but showed no fruit. Her knowledge of English history, enlarged by the special study of events affecting this country from the Peace of Amiens[36] down to the repeal of the Corn Laws in 1849, of which she possessed ample notes, would have formed a valuable contribution to our knowledge of times so eventful. Her observations on public men and public affairs were apt and convincing; and whilst rejoicing in the discomfiture of monopolies and shams of every kind,

"L'Aurora" by Guido Reni, 1613-1614

she hailed the legislation that tended to the material benefit and happier opportunities of the worthier industrial population. Common sense, a happy discrimination, and enlightenment, directed her opinions and counsel. She was far from being prone to indulge in conversation on matters of graver public interest except with well-tried friends. Not the slightest tincture of "blue-stockingism" prevailed in her composition; on the contrary, retiring manner and modesty of expression were her natural habit. Her sentiments were couched in a suggestive and persuasive tone, and rarely rose to the argumentative; yet, if needful, in discussion, she could maintain her own lines of thought with firmness and ability. Nor was she reticent on errors of commission, or any tendency to wrong-doing, manifested either by private individuals or by public officials, but an uncompromising foe to shabbiness of purpose and tergiversation.

There was no appearance of effort on the part of Miss Losh either in common narrative or in lengthened argument. Her thoughts flowed in an even stream, as continuously and consecutively as her own pulse; apparently attracting her listeners as much by her manner and clear measured tones of voice, as by the exactitude of her thoughts and the genuineness of her deductions. A stranger observing her reserve, and her calm, unostentatious, yet slightly constrained method of address, would experience a momentary frigidity in her presence; but this soon wore off as the conversationalist got awakened by the interest of the theme, and found a responsive listener.

Endowed so highly, she wanted but a larger share of self-esteem and love of approbation to enable her to rival any of her feminine contemporaries engaged in the paths of history and letters. She possessed a fair proportion of wit and a keen perception of the humorous, yet her tendency was more towards the threshold of philosophy than the boudoirs of sentimentality; and her writings indicated erudition and higher reasoning much more than poetic imagery.

Had Miss Losh been a Parisian by birth and education, her linguistic attainments, her

149

intellectual culture, her love of scientific progress and refined art, her criticisms so sound and logical, and her conversation so suggestive, would have endeared her to circles as brilliant as those presided over by Madame de Stael[37] and other celebrities, whose salons have formed the theme and admiration of so many historical writers.

Miss Losh possessed the delicate refinement and all that is attractive and characteristic of the high breeding of an English gentlewoman; yet she manifested manly thought and precision, and solidity of accomplishments, without the sacrifice of a single feminine grace. Her intellect was of no common order, and almost approached in power that of my friend "George Eliot,"[38] who now stands unrivalled in British literature: she had very much of the charm and brightness, if a less share of the penetrativeness, profundity of thought, and poetic eloquence, possessed by the author of "Romola."

Miss Losh greatly improved both the family mansion and property of Woodside. Her renovations of the former were of such extent as almost to dwarf the old ancestral home of the Loshes. To indulge her Italian fancies, she erected a Pompeian court as part of her gardenesque embellishments, and everywhere carried out the family penchant for trees and shrubs and flowers, and the beautifying of her domain. Few estates are so thickly planted, and nowhere in Cumberland does the same amount of arboreal growth prevail. The highroad through the Losh property to Wreay is bounded by hedges of hawthorn and holly, interspersed with the arbor-vitae, laurels, yews, laburnums, roses, honeysuckle, &c., making it the most charming drive around Carlisle. Silver firs and other pines of rare growth, but chiefly the oak, constitute natural avenues without formality - here the pyramidal elevation and graceful line, there the angular and drooping branches - giving to the long vista a natural Gothic through which the lights and shadows flicker in summer-time over alleys green. Everything around the abode partakes of the Losh character - the fences, the thatched cottage, or Swiss chalet of Pompeian pattern, nestling under huge trees, and secluded as a hermitage; even the gates are special in style and fastenings. Neatness, quaintness, and speciality rule out of doors and to aesthetic mind both aptly and well, inasmuch as they accord with the natural scenery around.

The hamlet and village of Wreay are also equally characteristic of Sara Losh's impress. The church she erected in 1842, worthy of a chapter by itself; the graveyard, with its yews and cedars and mournful shadowings, its mausoleum, its monumental obelisk, its quaint tombstones and devices, strike every visitor. All these works originated with Sara Losh - nay, more, they were designed, and developed, and completed by herself. She was the architect and superintendent of the works *ab initio*, and in most instances the moulder of the natural-history forms gracing the ecclesiastical building. Bound by no commonplace rules, and following none of the stereotyped lines of masonry, she directed the workmen in their operations from day to day. Like a master-mind, loving her work, she carried her church-building and other designs in her brain, and from the foundation to the finishing of the superstructure never had to undo what had been done according to her directions. As she only engaged country operatives, who had never shown the slightest feeling for art, she made her mouldings in clay, and then taught the mason how to work them in stone; and marvelously well did she succeed. The diverse forms - borrowed from botany, conchology, and other zoological divisions; from quaint mediaeval architecture and fossilised structures - to be found in the doorway, windows, and other parts of Wreay Church, are well done, and to Sara Losh is due the credit of their constructiveness.

In her occasional visits to Carlisle, Miss Losh became cognisant of the crowded state of the church burial-grounds, and being desirous to remedy this deplorable state of things, offered to give a field situated between the city and village of Upperby for a public cemetery. She made her proposal in the first instance to the Dean and Chapter, and on meeting with no encouragement in that quarter, tried the Corporation of Carlisle, but with as little avail. Indifference ruled the city magnates; the fear of losing burial fees or some vested rights held back the church dignitaries. Knowing the necessity of the step, she allotted an acre of land at Wreay for a burial-ground that should be available to all denominations of persons – a free gift to the public. This new cemetery was walled round, and planted with ivy and climbing shrubs; yews and arbor-vitae decorate the enclosure. Whilst considering the form of a mortuary chapel, the drifting dunes along the coast of Cornwall revealed in 1835 a long-lost church, the oldest in England, and traditionally ascribed to St Piran or Perran of the fifth, or some say the ninth, century[39]. The name of the present Perranzabuloe, the place of St Perran in the sand, supports the tradition. Miss Losh having obtained drawings, decided on reproducing "St Perran's Oratory" at Wreay. The building is 29 feet long by 16½ feet broad, and 13 feet high, and is entered by doors on the east and south. Around the interior of the oratory is a stone seat. Over the rude altar table is an extremely narrow window; a larger one admits light on the south side. The roof and doorways are modern, and the introduction of a palm-tree is evidently Miss Losh's own. To render everything complete, she erected a pretty cottage for the sexton in contiguity to the oratory, and furnished it with a garden.*

The grassy approach to the oratory, the simplicity of its structure, and the perfect solitude reigning around afford proofs of the lady's sympathetic feeling for the repose of the dead; and her larger sympathy for the interests of the living placed in proximity to crowded churchyards, and thereby liable to have their moral sense no less than their physical nature deteriorated. On this sanitary question, as on many others, Miss Losh showed large consideration and foresight. She was probably the first person in England to anticipate the extra-mural interment scheme of the Government; nay, her anticipation was so far ahead that neither the civic nor the ecclesiastical authorities of Carlisle could be persuaded to accept the important boon she wished to confer upon the inhabitants of the city.

As far as I can learn, the Wreay copy of the long-lost church, said to be the earliest church for Christian worship in the island, is the only one to be met with in England. The sea, it may be noted, engulfed a second church near to St Perran's some time in the last century.

Holding the memory of their father and mother in the highest regard, the sisters Losh sought to establish a permanent record of their affection in honour of their parents; and Sara, the leading mind, suggested the erection of an obelisk in Wreay Church burial-ground, a suggestion that had to be carried out by herself after her dear sister's death. Aware of the deep archeological interest attached to the ancient runic monument at Bewcastle[41], in Cumberland, and personally cognisant of its gradual decay, she wished a reproduction of this historic structure as an *in memoriam*. Accordingly, she obtained a large monolith, and caused a copy of the Bewcastle obelisk to be made as faithfully as circumstances would permit, and in this she was aided by the admirable drawings of her friend Mr. Howard[42] of Corby Castle, recorded in volume third of this series. But instead of imitating the effaced "Runes" on the west side of the obelisk, where the figures are depicted, she caused the following inscription to be made beneath the female figure and child : "Jehovah lux mea et salus mea est" ("The Lord is my light and my salvation," Ps. xxvii. i); and beneath the supposed saint the following: "Gratiam fac mihi: Deus, gratiam fac mihi nam ad te se recipit anima mea: et ad umbram alarum tuarum me recepturus sum" ("Be merciful unto me, 0 God, be merciful unto me; for my soul trusteth in Thee: and under the shadow of Thy wings shall be my refuge," Ps.lvii. i.) At the base of the column (west side): "Inumbret hoc signum consolia-tionis sepulchrum Joanniis Lossii et uxoris Isabellae. Salvi eatis, animae carissimae, per mediam umbram mortis. Avete in tempora refrigerii a conspectus Domini" (May this sign of consolation cast its shadow on the grave of John Losh and his wife Isabella. Souls well beloved, may you walk safe through the midst of the shadow of death. Farewell till the times of refreshing from the presence of the Lord.) On the south side of the obelisk, at its base, is the following elegant and touching record: "Hoc saxumt poni duae filiae sibi proposuerunt; una maestissima effecit", (Two daughters purposed that this stone should be set up; one performed it, greatly sorrowing.)

Katharine Isabella Losh died in February 1835, to the almost inconsolable grief of her sister, who to the end of her days brooded over this sad bereavement. Wishing to perpetuate, as far as sculptural art was available, the delightful form and visage of her devoted sister, as she had sketched her whilst seated on a rocky surface overlooking the Bay of Naples, Miss Losh engaged Mr D. Dunbar of Carlisle to carry out her views. She aided him so materially that the portrait statue became very much her own design, in the copying of which, in finely polished marble, the sculptor pretty fairly embodied the graceful sentiment so much solicited. The figure is seated, and almost entirely draped; the face is sweetly rendered, and a good likeness; the hair is dressed in Grecian form, and is partly shown in front of her neck and breast, over which the right arm is gracefully placed, whilst the left hand, upon which her eyes are intent, holds a fir-cone, a favourite emblem of Sara Losh's, as evidenced in many of her designs. At the base of the statue is the following deeply touching tribute by Sara to her sister: "Cathariua Isabella, soror placens*,' amabilis, piaque: semper mihi carissima eris: * *The word "placens" admits of other meanings; and my classic friend, Mr. Theodore Martin* cara nunc tua pallida imago" (Katharine Isabella, sweet sister, loving and pious, thou wilt ever be most dear to me; dear is thy pale image now.)

To protect the statue she erected in Wreay Churchyard a mausoleum, semi-Celtic or Druidical in character, if not partaking of the Attic form of Cyclopean architecture, consisting of large blocks of stone without an arch, mortar, or cement. The outer door of the building is of oak covered with copper, the inner of a rare black oak dug out of a neighbouring moss. Within the angles of the building are fine medallions of John and his wife, Isabella Losh, and also of George Losh.

Miss Losh took a large and varied interest in all matters pertaining to Cumberland and its ancient capital, and would gladly have aided in many ways to beautify it; and had she lived, would have rejoiced to see the restoration of the Cathedral[43] carried so far as it has been, though still incomplete. When the directors of the Newcastle and Carlisle Railway[44] decided on spanning the Eden at Wetheral, she suggested to them the erection of a bridge similar to the Pont du Gard, a few miles from Nimes, as calculated to harmonise well with the lofty banks of the river and the exquisitely-wooded scenery of Corby Castle. She made suitable drawings of her proposed plan, that found acceptance with Mr. Howard of Corby Castle and others of good taste; but railways were then in their infancy, and rough masonry rather than aesthetic embellishment ruled the general direction. To-day her views would probably have met with more acceptance even on utilitarian grounds.

Miss Losh built an infants' school at Wreay, and placed a worthy dame in charge of it. This school fell into disuse when the new Educational Act made it compulsory for girls and boys to be educated under the same roof. And to meet this view, she erected an entirely new school in 1830 - being aided to the extent £100, bequeathed by her aunt, Margaret Losh. Miss Losh carried her generosity further, and endowed the school with thirty acres of land, the rents or proceeds derived from which to be applied to the education of poor children

translates Horace's "placens uxor," "the winsome wife." From some reminiscences I am led to think that the interpretation of her inscription given above would have met with Miss Losh's approval.

* *The Chapel of Wreay having been totally neglected at the Reformation, twelve proprietors in the neighbourhood, styling themselves trustees, took upon themselves the direction of all affairs within the hamlet, and converted the chapel into a schoolhouse. These "twelve men" seem an embodiment of the ancient "folk-mote" of the Hundred, a kind of parochial remnant of the Witenagemote of the nation. Probably their functions extended to a surveillance of the cock-fighting and other pastimes for which Wreay was once famous, as the following paragraph from Carlyle's "Endowed Grammar Schools" (vol, i. p. 204) reveals:*

"A singular donation was made to the Wreay school by a Mr. Graham, of a silver bell weighing 2 oz upon which is engraved 'Wreay Chapple, 1655,' to be 'fought for annually by cocks'. About three weeks previous to that day the boys fixed upon two of their schoolfellows for captains, whose parents were able and willing to bear the expense of the approaching contest; and the master on his entering the school was saluted by the boys throwing up their hats, and the acclamation of 'Dux! Dux!' After an early dinner on Shrove Tuesday, the two captains,

in the adjoining townships. This endowment is held in trust by the TWELVE MEN of Wreay,* with whom rests the appointment of the schoolmaster, and the distribution of the Lowthian trusts, &c. She also erected a cottage for the schoolmaster on the model of one discovered at Pompeii, recorded on the Ordnance Survey maps of Cumberland as the "Pompeian Cottage."

The cost of erecting High Hesket School was mainly defrayed by Miss Losh, and the same may be said of Upperby School.

The dilapidated state of the old chapel at Wreay, in which the Loshes worshipped, induced Miss Losh to undertake the building of a new church. This, her largest effort, deserves a brief description, as exemplifying the catholicity of her views no less than her historical knowledge and architectural skill in all its originality and force.

WREAY CHURCH

The church erected by Miss Losh is founded on the Romanesque style, largely supplemented by her own ideas and thorough knowledge of church architecture. Not disposed to copy from any building or style *per se*, she designed an original church, consisting of baptistery, nave, and chancel or apse, with turret crowned by a Roman eagle.

The baptistery, nave, and pro-chancel measure in the interior about 46½ feet in length, by 28 feet in breadth; the height being in good ecclesiastical proportions. The apse is about 16 feet by 15 feet. The exterior walling is of square, rough-dressed stones, bearing some analogy to Roman work; the roof is covered with redstones or flags. The gable or western front is pierced with an arcade of small arches following the slope of the roof, features to be met with in Lombard and Rhenish churches, and notable in those of San Michele in Pavia, and the Duomo of Parma.

The entrance doorway is in the Lombard style, recalling that of Santa Maria della Piazza, Ancona; and is much admired. The boldly-carved hood moulding over the door is ornamented with the leaf and flower of the water-lily alternately; and the label mouldings terminate in bosses carved in the shape of pine-cones. The doorcase (interior) represents a gourd-plant, emblematic of the Old Testament as a preparation for, or entrance into, the

attended by their friends and schoolfellows, who were distinguished by blue and red ribbons, marched in procession from their respective homes to the village green, where each produced three cocks, and the bell was appended to the hat of the victor-in which manner it was handed down from one successful captain to another."

In 1836 the cock-fighting of Wreay was put down by the Rev. R. Jackson; in its place there is an annual hunt and the mayoralty, briefly noticed in vol. iii. p. 60 of this series. The noted bell of 1655, a parochial institution for 217 years, was stolen last year (1872) from the public house where the convivial meetings used to be held, and where it had so often graced the hats of "cocking champions," or the white nod of sham mayors.

New. This oaken carving was done by Miss Losh's gardener.

On entering the church, visitors are struck with the "dim religious light" as vastly too dim; this feeling, however, is but momentary, whilst the solemnity of the building gradually makes itself felt. Near to the entrance, on the right, is the Font, constructed of native alabaster, partly carved by Miss Losh herself, and presenting the zigzag moulding of the English Norman at the top, and curious Grecian fluting at the bottom, in excellent workmanship. It is also engraven with emblems – e.g. the lily, butterfly, vine, pomegranate, signifying in the eyes of ecclesiologists, purity, transition to a new life, the ineffable union betwixt Christ and His Church, and hope in immortality.* The cover of the font is silvered glass, on which appear, as if floating, lotus-flowers of native alabaster, mainly carved by Mr W. S. Losh.

On the left of the entrance door, and near the north wall of the church, hangs a Jewish lamp in front of one table of the Law; on the right, and against the south wall, the other table of the Law is above a bracket supported by the owl and cock-emblems of vigilance.

From the western platform, or more truly the baptistery, which is about seven feet in length, you descend by three steps to the body of the church, as you do in some Jewish synagogues; and on the right and left of these steps are pine-cones, on square pediments, viewed as emblematic of the passage through death to immortality.

The nave is about 34 feet in length; and the seats of the church are made of Woodside oak, and Spanish chestnut, obtained from Lowther Park after the January gale of 1839[45]; they are open, roomy, with sloping backs, and afford ample provision for kneeling, and show no ornamentation.

From the nave you ascend by three steps to the pro-chancel of six feet in length, on which stand the desks for the officiants. The desk to the south is an oaken eagle; that to the north is a pelican. The books are bound in wood, and those upon the eagle chained. Behind these desks stand two chairs[46] of antique character in place of chancel stalls, constructed of black oak obtained from a neighbouring peat-moss ; the backs of these chairs are formed by ebony panels from Italy, carved in bold relief with representations of the Nativity and the Epiphany. The arms of one of the chairs are supported by a carved griffin, the other by a butterfly form. On the south-east corner of the pro-chancel stands the pulpit, of bog-oak, supposed to be a natural tree-stem, but more probably cut in imitation of one of the calamites of the Coal-Measures. By the side of the pulpit, forming a support for a light or candle, is a palm-shaped tree formed of bog-oak.

Walcott's "Sacred Archaeology" is the authority for these explanations. It is well to note, however, that the emblems mentioned above are differently construed by different authorities, and that ecclesiologists are more disposed to assign a Christian meaning than to consider the mythological element so largely prevailing historically. The able and recondite work of my friend, Mr. Thomas Inman of Liverpool, entitled "Ancient Faiths embodied in Ancient Names," has opened out a vein of curious speculation that behoves the attention of those searching for larger interpretation of these emblems.

Above the pro-chancel arch is a wooden ledge, sustaining figures of angels playing on harps and other musical instruments, the figures alternating with pa1m-trees. On the wall below these, or rather to the north and south, are angels with outstretched wings, like those of the cherubim overshadowing the mercy-seat in the tabernacle.

From the pro-chancel you ascend by three steps to the apse or apsidal altar-place, about 16 feet long and 15 feet broad, which is surrounded by an arcade of fourteen pillars, with Romanesque capitals, adorned with quaint and emblematic carvings. The spaces between these pillars form thirteen sedilia, a direct architectural derivation from the Roman Basilica. The seven easternmost recesses arc pierced with openings which contain seven lamps of coloured glass symbolic of the seven works of the Spirit of God[47]; and thirteen of the small windows on a higher range are of native alabaster, pierced with forms derived from the fossilised ferns* of the Coal-measures of Northumberland, and defended from the outside by plates of glass. The natural-history embodiments were partly the work of Mr. W. S. Losh. Above these again is a string course, forming the base of the dome or roof of the apse, decorated with classic dentil ornaments.

In the chord of the apse stands the altar, which consists of a slab of green marble from Italy set in a wooden frame, and supported by two solid brass eagles standing on plinths of freestone, supported on a base carved with ears of wheat and clusters of grapes, symbolic to the Church of the Holy Eucharist. The altar candlesticks are of native alabaster carved in the shape of the lotus-flower.

At the north-west and south-west sides of the apse stand the Gospel and Epistle lights - bronze candelabra of Pompeian design, supporting lamps from Pompeii. These candelabra, when decorated with ivy at Christmas-tide, have a very pretty effect.

The pedalia, or foot-cloths, in front of the altar, are bear-skins; and bear-skins, according to Walcott's "Archaeology"[49], were used for the purpose in 1092 - possibly as votive offerings.

The stove[51] at the west end of the church is of iron, cast in the form of the stem of the sigillariae, as found in the lower Northumbrian Coal-Measures. On the antique stove in the east end stands a bronze holy-water pail[50], its rim bearing a Norman inscription;** it was brought from Normandy by Miss Losh and a standing pot for incense, according to post-Reformation custom (see "Hierurgia Anglicana," 1868, pp. 181-184).***

The windows of the nave are after the Romanesque Lombard character, those at the

*Among the fossilised ferns may be noted the neuropteris acuminata, Pecopteris heterophylla, Sphenopteris dilata, and Sphenophylyium Schlotheimii.
** The inscription runs thus: "Prie pour Palme. G. Glanville." There are also three curiously wrought designs on the pail: one supposed to represent the devil blowing a horn and ringing a bell; another may be a vine-dresser; the third is more problematic.
*** I am indebted for this reference, and much courteous aid in my inquiries respecting Wreay Church, to my friend the Rev. Thomas Lees, the vicar.

west end being on the outside adorned with various emblems - e.g., owl and dove for night and morning, the caterpillar, chrysalis, and butterfly, the Egyptian scarabeus, fossil shells, fir-cones, pomegranates, sunflowers, corallines, and poppies; some of these emblems are looked upon as significant of the transitional progress of the soul from a lower to a higher state of being. The upper lights at this west end are partly coloured and partly of alabaster, showing the cereal gramineae and clusters of grapes, already adverted to us as symbolic of the elements of the Lord's Supper.

The small circular-headed windows round the top of the apse are of a character usually found in Romanesque churches in Italy and on the Rhine; and the upper tier windows of the nave are of a similar character, but arranged in groups of threes. The windows of the nave are filled with quarry glass, the amber and ruby colours of which are brilliant. The central compartment of each group of upper tier windows, as well as those in the western gable, contain floral designs in coloured glass. One of these compartments at the east end, figuring the night-shade, is filled with glass gathered by Mr W. S. Losh in 1830, immediately after the July Revolution[53], from the ruins of the chapel in the palace of the Archbishop of Paris. The small slit windows on the north and south, to give light to the officiants, are copied from the old (fourteenth-century) church at Newton-Arlosh[54].

The roof of the church is open to the ridge, and is constructed of oak timber, massive, carved, and highly effective; the wood was obtained from the richly-planted lawn of Woodside.

The building, when complete in every way, cost Miss Losh £1200.

In describing the consecration of Wreay Church on the 1st December 1842, one of the local prints concluded its notice in the following words: "Although we arc aware that the unobtrusive and truly Christian character of that lady's benevolence makes her prefer to do good by stealth, it is only right to add that the inhabitants [of Wreay parish] are wholly indebted to the munificent liberality of Miss Losh of Woodside for the erection of this elegant and convenient place of worship."

In designing Wreay Church, Miss Losh apparently wished to recognise the germinal stages of religion, and the unlettered worship of man, as well as the historic churches pertaining to the monotheistic idea - the grandest religious idea to which the human mind has as yet attained. Imbued with a special knowledge of architecture, and no less prompted by a true archaeology, she founded an ecclesiastical structure, the significance of which was hardly comprehended by Bishop Percy[52] and his episcopate supporters assembled on the day of its consecration. This edifice aims correctly enough to supply the wants of Christian worship according to the rites of the Established Church of England; but it is not less aptly but largely emblematic of more ancient faiths, and the varied graftings of these onto modern beliefs. The progressive forms and types of sacred worship are traced from the earliest manifestations of the Judaic and Christian standards, down to the post-Reformation period.

Cognisant of the Religious Cults that have prevailed in the world as the expression of the innate desire in man to penetrate the mysterious workings of the one eternal, all-pervading Spirit of nature, crystallized into various forms suited to the mental constitution of the peoples who embrace them, Miss Losh seems to have taken a broad survey of the historic past. Thus her illustrations drawn from the fossil world may have been offered as a tribute of acknowledgment to nature-worship, or the first idealistic breathings towards the infinite and the unknown; and in her tracings from the primitive and mysterious through the different ascents to prophetic religions evincing man's morality touched by devotion, she presents a kind of pantheistic temple, in which Jew and Gentile, Rationalist and Ritualist, may find something congenial to his taste and more or less tantamount to a support of his faith. She mingles the antediluvian world and that of external nature with the adornments of the churches of the East, in which Paganism and Deism, the Law and the Prophets, prefigure the forms, the affinities, and the antagonisms of the newer developments of our race.

The atmospheric light is seen passing through the fern forms of the antediluvian jungle and striking the lotus-flower, the emblem of receptivity and reproduction adorning the modern altar, itself a sun of hope to the Christians; and this light again, in its transmission through the seven-coloured media, symbolic of the seven works of the Spirit of God, gives rise to the idea of transition from one sphere to another higher in degree of the worship of the creative principle acting upon chaos, till it eventually culminates in the Christian formula.

In the caterpillar, the chrysalis, and perfect butterfly, you realise the genesis, the growth, and maturity of life; whilst other forms typify mortality, the mid shades, and immortality beyond. The observer may trace the indications of the alpha and the omega of organisation, in the simplest of living forms, blending with the highest of entities terrestrial and assumed heavenly.

The device on one of the capitals in the apse is a bird eating an amphibious animal like a frog, probably meant for the sacred Ibis consuming the product of an earlier age, that of chaotic mud; and if divested of this interpretation, simulating the gradatory flow of organic development, itself pointing to a grand and substantial basis of a natural theology that seeks affinity with the reign of law and a great Lawgiver. On other capitals are clusters of grapes, emblematic of exuberance; and scripturally woman has been compared to the fruitful vine, around whom as a *bona dea* may be associated the goddess of nature.

In the seraph, the open lotus-flowers and pomegranate, the seeds of which fruit recall Persephone's experience of Hades, and open out new fields of thought, Nature in her broader genetic aspects is clearly indicated. And as the voluptuous language of the Song of Solomon has been rendered typical of Christ and His Church, so have the mythological attributes been made subservient to the call of modern ecclesiologists, with or without wisdom in the choice and adaptation. However this may be, the ornamentative forms of Wreay Church - be they foliage, flowers, or fruit, be they insects, or reptiles, birds or beasts - portend creation quickened by one Spirit, and that Spirit pervading the universe *ad infinitum*. Coming down to the historic period, you observe a transcript of Egyptian forms prior in date to, as well as those belonging to, Solomon's temple and the Jewish synagogue, then the pagan basilica and curial chair transformed into a Christian church, with its thirteen sedilia for the Founder and His disciples, or the Bishop and his clergy; and these again modified to suit the wants of "modernism," or, if you choose, the prevailing sentiment of these latter days.

Miss Losh's insight into the past is marked by largeness of view, and a spacious conception of human worship through its initiatory stages of fetishisms, mystic longings and superstitions, onward to the more modern interpretation that seeks solace in churches and an ordained priesthood. Unbiassed by dogma, she sought in her novel construction the general wants of mother Church in and around Wreay. At the same time, she could not deny the higher instincts of her own nature, and the pleasure of carrying out an architectural design of original character, in the hope of indoctrinating others with sentiments and aspirations analogous to her own. She wished to raise the parochial mind to a higher contemplation of the Deity attended by devotional feeling, than was likely to be engendered by bare walls, cabined seats, and rude masonry; and in doing so, manifested her own aesthetic taste and regard for the historical of all churches - be that regard derived from the decorative emblems of an Eastern temple, the bold moulding of the Norman, or the incense-serving stand of the Tudor-Elizabethan era. And curious it is to see how she wove the prehistoric, and the mythologies of primordial man, with modern Christian doctrine that aspires to ennoble all. There is unity of purpose throughout the work, showing the development of the different Cults, from the time of Osiris and his Nilotic nymphs, through the days of the wise King, bright in his polygamy and home virtues, down to the monogamic non-virtuous Anglo-Saxon, accredited with representing the latest phase of civilization! The lady of Woodside, in giving full scope to her powers, seems to have approached the idea of race and faith determining the character of the temple; that as Olympian morality was reflected in the Parthenon, the noblest and purest art structure the world ever saw, so did medieval Christendom evoke York Minster; and Commonwealth Puritanism find its proper habitat in the meagre structures not ill defined by George Fox, the Quaker, as "steeple houses."

Guided in part by her penchant for archaeology, and the belief that her ancestral name was Arlosh,* she took much interest in the tower** of the ancient church at Newton-Arlosh, in Holm-Cultram, and on one of her visits was not a little chagrined to find the villagers carting away the stones of the ruined mediaeval edifice. To arrest this iconoclasm she wrote to Bishop Percy[52], offering to build an Episcopal church favourable to the incorporation of the ruins of the early fourteenth-century one. The Bishop rejoiced at this proposal, as a church was much needed; and parochial opinion being directed to the subject, steps were taken in furtherance of Miss Losh's scheme, upon which, it is said, she spent several hundred

* It should have been noted in a previous page, introducing the family history of the Loshes, that in the list of Cmnberland `gentry returned by the Commissioners 12 Henry VI., the name of Arlosh occurs along with others whose continuance became more or less doubtful after the year 1500.

159

pounds. No one who has seen Wreay Church can visit the new church at Newton-Arlosh without at once detecting the Losh architecture throughout its design[53].

The place was originally Arlosh, and only received the additional Newton-Arlosh when the inhabitants of Skinburness were driven by the inroads of the Solway Firth[54] to take up their quarters further inland, adding so greatly to the population of Arlosh as to require a market early in the fourteenth century. Newton-Arlosh, defined as the new town near the marsh, is the mother Church of the Abbey Holme, whilst the Abbey Church ranged with the old conventual establishment; this has been evidenced of late years in the clergymen of the said Abbey Church having "to read themselves in" amid the ruins of the ancient church of Newton-Arlosh.

Miss Losh practised a large benevolence, and in a most catholic spirit, knowing neither creeds nor politics in the distribution of her bounties. Infirmaries, schools, blind asylums, and other charitable institutions, found in her a good friend. Her subscriptions were large, as the public lists showed; but her private charity was even more extensive, and meant to be unknown beyond the recipients. The last act of her life was a donation of £70 to a school at Upperby, without which aid the school might have remained in abeyance for some time. All her spendings at home were upon her friends and a handsome hospitality; upon herself literally nothing but good books. Her servants were well cared for during their service, and pensioned off and rendered comfortable in their old days. You rarely dined at Miss Losh's table without meeting superior-minded company in various walks of life; and it may be mentioned, as exemplifying the catholicity of her regards, that I have seen around her social board Unitarians and Episcopalians, Catholics and Christians unattached. Visitors enjoyed staying at Woodside, where the active and ardent mind of a gracious hostess showed

" A fancy pregnant with resource and scheme
To cheat the sadness of a rainy day,"[55]

however much it clouded the landscape of the neighbouring vale; and might well commend

"The consummate harmony serene
Of gravity and elegance, diffused
Around the mansion and its whole domain;
Not, doubtless, without help of female taste
And female care."[56]

Miss Losh was specially mindful of the interests of those in a humbler position of life, seeking their advancement and well-being as if she revered,

"And would preserve as things above all price,
The old domestic morals of the land
Her simple manners, and the stable worth
That dignified and cheered a low estate."[57]

As illustrating her ability to cope with difficulties of no ordinary kind, and her sympathy with those who stood in need of friendly aid, Miss Losh took up the case of a poor

160

woman involved in a lawsuit, and unable to employ a lawyer; and after sifting all the evidence, pro and con, established data necessary for the defence of her client's claims. These she set forth in so lucid a manner that the plaintiff's solicitor viewed them as incontrovertible, and therefore advised his client to withdraw his action.

> "Observant, studious, thoughtful, and refreshed,
> By knowledge gathered up from day to day;
> Thus had she lived a long and innocent life,"[58]

in the enjoyment of tolerable if not robust health. Though liable to bronchitis for a couple of years or more, it was not till March 1853, when the biting east winds seized upon a frame somewhat debilitated by a few days illness and the growing despondency of age, that she showed signs of decadence. The last hours of this good lady, witnessed by myself, were calm and dignified; and to her the end of all things came on the morning of the 29th March 1853. Her remains were interred in the Losh enclosure of the Wreay Chapel burial-ground, by the side of her much-loved sister and Aunt Margaret. A rectangular stone covers the grave of the two sisters, upon a smooth surface of which is inscribed: " Katharine Isabella Losh, died February, 1835, aged 47. Sarah Losh, died March 29, 1853. In vitae divisae,, in morte conjunctae " (Parted in life; in death united). "Lord, let Thy mercy lighten upon us." Under the inscription is represented a large coralline and scallop-shell, which the good lady herself used to associate with the pilgrimage through life.

On the 19th April 1853 the villagers of Wreay planted two lime-trees on the village green in memory of Sara and Katharine Isabella Losh. All the scholars of both schools attended and assisted in planting the trees, being made specially cognisant of how much they owed to Sara Losh.

The villagers of Upperby also testified their unanimous regard for the memory of their great benefactress by planting a lime-tree in contiguity to the schoolhouse, which she had been mainly instrumental in erecting. Both these neighbourly doings were a pretty tribute to one who had ever shown a love of trees and the beauteous in nature.

Editorial Notes on Lonsdale

Lonsdale's own notes are printed at the foot of the page.

1) William Wordsworth: "The Excursion: Book First: The Wanderer", lines 90-94.

2) Rev. William Gaskin: born 1751; ordained deacon as assistant curate to Rector of Caldbeck, 1777, priest 1780; acting schoolmaster Wreay, succeeded Joseph Parker 1783; died 1832, aged 81, "Perpetual Curate of Wreay and Walton".

3) William Paley (1743 – 1805): Dean of Carlisle, Christian apologist, utilitarian, and philosopher.

4) Dean Isaac Milner (1750--1820): Dean of Carlisle, Lucasian Professor of Mathematics in Cambridge, divine, engineer, chemist and friend of William Wilberforce.

5) Rev. Dr. Carlyle (1758-1804): orientalist, accompanied Lord Elgin to Constantinople.

6) Sir Joseph Gilpin (1745-1833): of Scaleby Castle, distinguished army medical officer.

7) Dr Heysham (1753-1834): Medical Doctor. Compiled the Carlisle Bills of Mortality, and later Life Tables which proved of great importance to Life Insurance Companies; founded the Carlisle Dispensary. The subject of a long biography by Lonsdale.

8) Archibald Cochrane, ninth Earl of Dundonald (1749-1831): Chemist and agriculturist.

9) Sir John Leslie (1766-832): distinguished mathematician, chemist and physicist

10) Blamire family of the Oaks. A local family in the Losh circle, closely involved in radical politics. Both William and Jane were the subject of short memoirs by Lonsdale.

11) The Warwicks of Warwick Hall. Sarah Losh's uncle and family. They changed their name from Bonner to Warwick when they inherited the estate. Warwick Hall is about five miles east of Carlisle.

12) The Grahams of Low House: a branch of the Graham family of Netherby Hall, Longtown.

13) Thomas Carrick: English miniature painter. Born in 1802 at Upperby, died in 1875.

14) David Dunbar (1782 -1866): sculptor, a pupil of Francis Chantrey.

15) Baron Dr. Carl (Karl) Ludwig von Reichenbach (1788-1869): chemist, metallurgist, naturalist, spiritualist and philosopher, a member of the prestigious Prussian Academy of Sciences.

16) Sir Walter Scott. The Harraby gibbet that is so memorable in the latter part of "The Heart of Midlothian" is within three miles of Woodside.

17) Edward George Earl Bulwer-Lytton, 1st Baron Lytton (1803–1873): English novelist, playwright, and politician.

18) Adriaen van Ostade (1610 – 1685): a Dutch genre painter.

19) William Makepeace Thackeray (1811– 1863): regarded by many of his contempories as the leading English novelist.

20) A small town in the Savoy near Chambery.

21) The sunday before Ascension Day, when the priest would bless the crops.

22) St. Bruno (about 1048 - 1123): Founder of the Carthusian Order.

23) From 1731 until 1740 Rousseau lived with

24) Madame de Warens at her country home,

25) Les Charmettes, near Chambery in the Savoy.

26) "He dared to consecrate his life to glory and to truth and was always persecuted by himself and envy."

27) An ancient city in Perugia on foothills of the Apennines.

28) Small town in central Italy.

29) Virgil: Aeneid Book vii: "From land a gentle breeze arose by night, / Serenely shone the stars, the moon was bright, / And the sea trembled with her silver light." Dryden's translation.

30) Pompeii was rediscovered in 1748.

31) Diomides:Villa of Diomedes in the Street of Tombs; an extensive garden enclosed by a portico 36yd. long.

32) Founded in 7th century B.C. by Greek city of Sybaris, originally called Poseidonia. One of the best preserved groups of Greek temple buildings. South of Pompeii.

33) A territory in Italy that included Paestum.

34) Antonio Allegri da Correggio (1489 – 1534): foremost painter of the Parma school of the Italian Renaissance,

35) Guido Reni (1575 - 1642): Italian painter of the High Baroque.

36) The Treaty of Amiens was signed on March 25, 1802, between France and the United Kingdom. The Peace lasted one year.

37) Anne Louise Germaine de Staël (1766 – 1817): French-speaking Swiss author living in Paris. The great intellectual and literary hostess of her age.

38) Pen name of Mary Anne Evans (1819 – 1880).

39) Perranzabuloe - south-east of Perranporth in Cornwall.

41) The 7th century cross at Bewcastle in North-east Cumbria.

42) His drawings were published in "Archaeologia" in 1802.

43) Ewan Christian restored Carlisle Cathedral in the 1850s.

44) Built between 1830 and 1838. James Losh was on the board until his death.

45) Lowther Park - the estate of the very wealthy Lord Lowther, Earl of Lonsdale, to the south of Penrith.

49) These chairs have been stolen.

47) "Revelation 4:5" "And from the throne proceeded lightnings, thunderings, and voices. Seven lamps of fire were burning before the throne, which are the seven Spirits of God."

48) The stove is missing.

49) "Sacred Archaeology; a Popular Dictionary of Ecclesiastical Art and Institutions, from Primitive to Modern Times by Walcott", Mackenzie E. C. London: L. Reeve and Co. 1868.

50) Now in Carlisle Cathedral Treasury.

51) "HIERURGIA ANGLICANA Documents and Extracts illustrative of The Ceremonial of the Anglican Church after the Reformation edited by members of the Ecclesiological late Cambridge Camden Society, A.D. 1848." reprinted 1868.

52) Bishop of Carlisle (1826-56).

53) The church was considerably altered in 1895 and there is now little sign of Sarah Losh's work.

54) In 1305.

55) Wordsworth: "The Excursion: Book VII: The Churchyard among the Mountains", lines 117 - 122.

56) Wordsworth: "The Excursion: Book VIII: The Parsonage", lines 534-538.

57) Wordsworth: "The Excursion: Book VIII: The Parsonage", lines 235-241.

58) Wordsworth: "The Excursion: Book I: The Wanderer", lines 394-397.

From "Wreay" by Canon Hall

CHAPTER V: SARAH LOSH

The Wreay of to-day owes very much of what is distinctive and interesting in it to Sarah Losh, of Woodside. She was the daughter of that John Losh who acted as sword-bearer to the first Mayor of Wreay. He was a noteworthy personage for other and more important reasons. He was educated at Sedbergh and Trinity College, Cambridge, a good linguist, chemist, and mechanic. He travelled much abroad before settling down as the Squire of Woodside. He was an intimate friend of the Howards of Corby Castle and Greystoke, and the Curwens of Workington. He not only largely developed his property at Wreay, but also, along with his brother and the Earl of Dundonald, established chemical works near Newcastle, which contributed much to the prosperity of that city and of his own family. Dr. Lonsdale, in the fourth volume of Cumberland Worthies, gives a full account of the Loshes, and devotes one long chapter to the life and character of Sarah Losh. She was born in 1785 and baptised at St. Cuthbert's, Carlisle, in which city the family had a house. Her only brother, Joseph, was of weak intellect.

She inherited the Woodside Estates and the Walker Alkali Works on the death of her father, in 1814. She had one sister, Katharine Isabella, two years younger than herself; they were devoted to each other. They went to school together at Bath and London, traveled together in France and Italy, and lived together at Woodside; neither of them married. Dr. Lonsdale, who knew them both, describes Sarah as "quiet, humorous, and intellectual" - Katharine as "hearty and vivacious." Sarah was the more beautiful of the two, and regarded as the belle of the Assize Balls at the Coffee House in Carlisle. She had also the greater abilities. She could read with ease Latin and Greek, French and Italian, and took an interest in art and some forms of science. She was a great planter of trees, and to her the road through the Woodside property from Brisco to Wreay owes much of its beauty. The death of her sister, in 1835, was a great blow to her. In her memory she supplied troughs to a roadside well at Roughton Ghyll on the Southwaite road, and erected a stone canopy above with the inscription, "Katharine Well." She also had a marble statue, executed by David Dunbar, of Carlisle, representing her sister seated, gazing intently at a fir cone which she holds in her left hand. This figure she placed in a mausoleum built of rough stones in a plot of ground immediately adjoining Wreay Churchyard. Underneath is the inscription: " Catherina Isabella, soror placens, amabilia piaque: semper mihi carissima eris: cara nunc tua pallida imago," which may be translated, "Catherine Isabella, sweet, lovely, sisterly sister; always wilt thou be most dear to me; dear too now is thy pale lifeless image."

On the interior walls of the mausoleum are also marble medallion portraits of their father and mother, and some other members of the Losh family.

Another record of her grief is contained in the inscription upon the base of a monolith in the same enclosure: "Hox saxum poni duae filiae sibi proposuerunt: una maestissima effecit," "Two daughters made the plan of putting up this stone; one only carried it out in great grief."

The stone is in most respects a copy of the famous Saxon cross at Bewcastle, the earliest and finest of the pre-Norman monuments Cumberland. Its most probable date is

A.D. 671. A full description of it will be found in the Victoria History of Cumberland, Vol. I, pp. 254-257, and a discussion of the meaning of its Runic inscription on pp. 277-8. The north, east, and south faces of the Wreay cross are copied exactly from that at Bewcastle, with the exception of the omission of some narrow lines of runes. On the west and principal face changes have been made. The central figure is the same - our Lord robed as a priest, with a halo surrounding His head, and right hand uplifted in blessing. So also is the lowest of the three figures - a man carrying a spear in his right hand, and lifting a hawk from its perch on to his lcft wrist. This is supposed to be meant as a portrait of King Alchfrith, in whose memory the monument was set up. The highest figure is asserted by antiquaries to represent St. John carrying a lamb, but the details are not very plain, and in the Wreay copy it has been replaced by a Virgin and Child. In place of the Runes, on this side are the following Latin quotations from the Psalms, "Jehovah lux mea et salus mea est" ("The Lord is my light and my salvation"), "Gratiam fac mihi: Deus, gratiam fac mihi: nam ad to se recipit anima mea: et ad umbram alarum tuarum me recepturus sum." ("Be merciful unto me, O God, be merciful unto me; for my soul trusteth in Thee, and under thc shadow of Thy wings, shall be my refuge").

Below, on this side of the base of the obelisk, is the inscription, showing that it was meant as a memorial of her parents :- "lnumbret hoc signum consolationis sepulchrum Joannis Lossii et uxoris Isabellae. Salvi eatis, animas carissimae, per mediam umbram mortis. Avete in tempora refrigerii a conspectu Domini" (May this sign of consolation cast its shadow upon the tomb of John Losh and his wife, Isabella. May you go safe, dearest souls, through the midst of the shadow of death. Fare ye well until the times of refreshing shall come from the presence of the Lord). The monument at Bewcastle has lost its top, and a cross has been placed on that at Wreay.

In the same plot of ground, surrounded by a dwarf curb, there is a pine tree. On the wall at one side of it stands a giant cone carved in stone, with this inscription below:-"This Khelat Pine is planted in memory of Wm. Thain, Major of the 33rd, and was raised from seed transmitted by him to England. He perished in the fatal Pass of Coord Cabul, esteemed and lamented by all who knew him." Although the inscription refers to another bereavement, it takes us back to the girlhood of Sarah and Katharine, for William Thain was a little boy at Wreay School when they were big girls - he was about six years younger than Katharine. I do not know how he came to be living at Wreay, or what were his connections with the Losh family. From an obituary notice of him in a Newcastle paper, in which a reference is made to the many warm friends which he had there, it seems that he came from those parts, but as a child he lived with farmers at Wreay, named Bewley. One Joseph Bewley was made one of the Twelve men in 1791, and when he died his son succeeded him as such in 1803. It is this younger Joseph Bewley who is the writer of the letter here given. An old Latin grammar is still preserved by Joseph Bewley's descendents, in which there is the inscription, "Wreay School. William Thain's Book, 1802." They also have the ribbon of his Waterloo medal, and the letter here copied. It has an interesting history. It was written in 1814 to Thain when he was a young officer, about eighteen years old, and it was returned to the writer by the War Office upon his death, in 1842, after a distinguished career. He had been aide-de-camp in India to General Elphinstone, who in his will left a legacy to "the sister of my dear and ever-to-be-lamented friend, Major Thain." So all through his career he had preserved this letter from Wreay, and the pine cone which he sent to the Miss Loshes shows that he also kept in touch with the place in other ways. His Latin grammar is proof that, Wreay School was able to supply a good education, long before Education Acts were passed, and Mr. Bewley's letter is evidence that farmers as well as military officers profited by it, and gives us also a peep into the life of Wreay a hundred years ago.

"Wreay, 16th June, 1814.

"My dear William,

"I received your letter dated Viesal, 21st April, informing me of your destination for Cork, where I hope by this time you have arrived in safety and in health. We were much alarmed for your safety in that unfortunate failure at Bergen-up-Zoom, but we were not kept long in suspense, as we had a regular detail from Sir Thomas Graham, wherein particular praise was bestowed upon the 33rd and 55th, and I never heard of any blame imputed to your regiment in the retreat, but on the contrary mention was made of the gallant and good conduct with which it was effected. I also received a line from you dated from Yarmouth Roads, and I suppose that your letters have all arrived safe.

"Believe me, my dear William, it has and always will be the greatest pleasure to me to hear from you, and I hope that should your regiment be ordered for America, the correspondence will be allways kept up; where a new scene will open to you, and where you will see human nature unadorned with the arts of refinement, and a country in a measure as it came from the hand of the great Creator. What a field for reflection! and I see no reason why a man may not be a Soldier and a moral Philosopher - of both which I hope you will profitt, for we have already heard honourable mention of you, and I expect that you will continue to make such improvements as time and opportunity will permit.

"Henry Gill died in the month of January 1813. Miss Bewley my sister died on the 2nd Feb, following. Mrs. Robley of Woodside died June following, and your much respected friend Mr. John Losh of Woodside died in the month of March 1814. His loss will be much felt in this neighbourhood. The two Miss Loshes continue at Woodside with little alteration in the family, except that Joseph is come to Mr. Gaskin's with a person appointed to take care of him.

"Mrs. Gaskin has brought her husband a son, whose name is John. Mr. Michael Sewell of St. Anthony was married to Grace Bell of Lowhurst in the spring of 1813, who has brought her husband a son and heir. Mr. Thomas Fell was married to Miss Bell about a month ago. John Bell has gone as clerk to his brother, and Miss Jane has gone to keep her brother's house. What a sudden alteration in that family.

"Jemmy Longrigg is married to Miss Sally Slack, who has brought him a son. Old David keeps the corner chair, and old Betty the landlady is as rough as ever.

"I was laid up in rheumatic fever for about seven weeks last summer. I suffered much and have not yet wholly recovered the use of arms. You will forgive me not answering your letters as regularly as I might, but I will be more dutifull for the future, and I see no harm in adressing your last to my daughter. Miss Margaret joins Mrs. Bewley in our best comp. to you, and believe me, dear William,

" I remain your sincere and affectionate friend,

"Lieu L. Lieu.

" P.S. Should you receive this in due time, and delay not, you may possibly hear from me again before you leave Cork.

"Lieu Lieu."

The signature "Lieu Lieu" I take to be the childish name given by W. Thain to Joseph Bewley when he first came to Townhead Farm. Wreay Village and School ought not to forget that a Wreay schoolboy fought and was wounded at Waterloo, and gave his life in defence of that north-west frontier of India, which has cost the British Empire so much to maintain from that day to this.

A cone became one of Miss Losh's favourite emblems. Cones terminate the dripstones over the west door of the Church which she built, and appear in the carvings of the windows above. The door lock is carved in the shape of cones. The nave is entered between two large cones of alabaster, a cone forms the centre ornament of each of the large beams of the roof, and a cone is also carved on the gravestone which covers both her sister and herself. It is probable that the form became dear to her, not only on account of its connection with Major Thain, but because she regarded it as an emblem of life preserved through apparent death. The dry cone, which seemed so dead, came to her over many thousand miles, but bore in it the little seed from which she was able to raise the living tree.

I have been told that another form which she introduces frequently in the Church building - an arrow - is due to the fact that Major Thain was killed by an Afghan arrow.

Miss Losh built a dames' infant school at Wreay (now known as Wreay Syke Cottage), and rebuilt, the old School on the Village Green. She built also a cottage for the schoolmaster, of a type similar to the houses of Pompeii, which were then being excavated. In the Ordnance Survey Maps it appears under the name of "Pompeian Cottage." She gave some lands, of which the rents were to go to pay for the school fees of children living outside the ancient township of Wreay, in the neighbourhood of Woodside. She gave and laid out a piece of ground as a Cemetery, built a mortuary chapel there, and adjoining it, a cottage for the Clerk. Her chief work for Wreay was the building of the present Church. She did much also for the restoration of Newton Arlosh Church.

After the sister's death she lived a life of comparative retirement at Woodside, in a barely-furnished room, though she still took an interest in literature and study, and was generous in helping her neighbours and supporting good works. When I came to Wreay some of the older residents still remembered her in her black cottage bonnet and long black cloak, often to be seen in the road between Woodside and Wreay. She died in 1853, and is laid in the Losh burial enclosure in Wreay Churchyard, by the side of her sister, one large rough block of stone covering both graves, on which are the inscriptions:

"Katharine Losh, died February, 1835, aged 47.

Sarah Losh, died March 29th, 1853.

In vita divisae, in morte conjunctae.

(In life divided, in death united.)

Lord let thy mercy lighten upon us."

CHAPTER VI: THE CHURCH

A CHAPEL must have existed at Wreay in the days of Edward the Second, for Bishop Halton, in 1319, permitted a Chaplain there "to attend divine offices" on condition that he resided within the Chapelry. In post-Reformation times there was a building which served both as Chapel and School House. There was no graveyard attached, nor any celebrations of Holy Communion, baptism, or marriages in it. In 1739, after some improvements, it was consecrated by Bishop Fleming. An addition had been made to the endowment of the benefice. The newly-appointed reader/schoolmaster, Joseph Parker, had been ordained deacon at the end of the previous year. A font was then placed in the chapel, which may still be seen in the present Churchyard, to the left of the west door, with the date upon it of 1738. Burials began to take place in the adjoining graveyard, at all events not later than 1750, when the Registers begin, but there was still no celebration of Holy Communion. That would follow in 1763, when Joseph Parker was ordained priest. The Chapel was never licensed for marriages. This was the structure which was replaced by the present building. Miss Sarah Losh has herself left an account of the circumstances which led to its erection, and the conditions under which she undertook the work.

The following are extracts from her memorandum upon the subject: "In the year 1840 the old Chapel at Wreay was found to be in a very dilapidated condition, the slate was much broken, the timber of the roof was in a state of dangerous decay, and the walls were in many places mouldy and green . . . A Committee having been formed for the restoration of the edifice, it was resolved to apply to the proper authorities for leave to remove it to a fresh spot, where it would be unencumbered by graves. This plan was approved by the Bishop and by the Chancellor of the Diocese, and by the Dean and Chapter of Carlisle, who, as patrons of the living, agreed to give £30 for the re-building of the chancel, that being the sum estimated for replacing it exactly as it then stood. With this aid I offered to furnish a new site for the Chapel, and to defray all the expenses of its re-erection, on condition that I should be left unrestricted as to the mode of building it. Mrs. M. Losh [i.e, Miss Margaret Losh, Sarah Losh's paternal aunt] and Mrs. A. Bonner [then living at Brisco Cottage, and most probably her maternal aunt] both kindly gave me, the former £50, the latter £100 [these sums were afterwards increased to £100 and £145) towards this work, and Mrs. Bonner presented us with the coloured windows, the brass eagles, &c. The destruction of an ancient structure, however necessary, must always afford cause for regret, but the Chapel at Wreay had apparently little claim to respect, either in an antiquarian or an architectural point of view. The walls were low and without any regular foundation, and although of considerable thickness, they displayed but indifferent masonry.

In the process of demolition, however, a small narrow door was discovered near the eastern end of the south wall. It forms the entrance of the new cript, and is a specimen of the flat headed corbel arch, so common in the time of Edward 1st. The plot of ground on which the Chapel now stands, was anciently part of the common belonging to the township; by the proprietors of which, on the enclosure of Wreay Common, it was hedged to afford a cow grassing for the Clerk. This outer enclosure formed an irregular belt of more or less breadth surrounding the Chapel yard on every side. It was made over to me by the Township in 1836, in exchange for another piece of land for the Clerk, thus enabling me to improve the appearance of the place by planting it with ever-greens, and also to rebuild with a little additional space, the wall of the Chapel yard, which had almost wholly disappeared. Subsequently it gave me the means of affording a new site for the Chapel. The ground was very uneven, and had formerly several pools of water, on which when frozen, the school boys skated. On levelling this place, the water gushed up, and filled the new dug foundation so rapidly, that it was necessary to fill it up with stones, and to commence further to the eastward. This water was drained off at a low level, and conveyed underneath the Chapel floor, in a large drain through the cript, where it received the water from the shallow drains made outside the Chapel walls. From the cript the large drain takes a north-easterly direction across the outer garth, where it is joined by the main drain from the new and old part of the Chapel yard. After this, it is carried underneath the public road and through the orchard opposite, whence there is a good descent for it down the bank. To secure the dryness of the Chapel floor, the flags were raised on dwarf walls, with the exception of the platform at the entrance, which is raised on dry stone chippings. With regard to the old materials of the fabric, the stones and flags were by agreement used by the builder.

The old pews were interposed betwixt the slates and the wood ceiling. The Communion Table is preserved in the cript.. The bell gable has been placed by the pond at the roadside to remain as a relic of the former Chapel. [This pond is known as the "Bell Well" on the road leading to High Wreay.] The unpolished mode of building adhered to in the new Chapel most approximates to early Saxon or modified Lombard, which was preferred to a more improved style, as less expensive and elaborate."

Miss Losh also left very minute accounts showing how much was paid for everything used in the course of building and for the labour employed. The total cost was £1,088 10s. 4d. This included £150 as the estimated value of oak cut at Wood Bank and Woodside, but not certain gifts such as two ebony panels from Paris, bronze eagles supporting the Holy Table, books bound in wood, and the angels above the chancel arch and on each side of it. There is no payment of an architect. Miss Losh was her own architect and designed every detail of the Church as well as its general plan. The work was carried out by the village masons and builders, named Hindson, the son, William, being responsible for the stone-carving. I have heard it stated, but have not been able to secure confirmation of the statement, that she sent him to Naples for some months, to see something of Italian architecture, and the excavations at Pompeii, and have instruction in stone-carving. Miss Losh sketched or modelled the various ornaments and he reproduced them in stone. The wood-carving was chiefly done by Mr. Scott, living at Dalston.

It is not plain whether Miss Losh, by "the unpolished mode of building," refers to the masonry or the architecture. The walls are of stone with a rough finish-not ashlar work. The style of architecture, if it is that which "approximates to early Saxon or modified Lombard," might also with equal truth be described as that of a basilica, such as would have been found in a small Greek or Roman city in the first century of the Christian era. These basilicas were built for civil purposes, to serve as courts of law, markets, or places of assembly. The earliest buildings erected for Christian worship would be of the same type. Its simplest form is that of Wreay Church - a plain rectangular nave, without aisles, with an apse at one end.

Surrounding the Church are grass terraces, quite free from graves. The old graveyard lies to the north. In its centre, marked by some yew trees, is the site of the Chapel which was demolished when the present Church was built.

On a grass plot to the right of the pathway, leading to the Church door, is a sun-dial, round the base of which is inscribed, "Do to-day's work to-day."

The doorway is a semi-circular headed arch of three members, the outer and the inner filleted, that between them carved with water-lily flowers. The dripstone above the arch is carved with water-lily leaves and flowers alternately, with cone terminals.

Above the door are three windows, surrounded by stone carvings. The centre one shows a chrysalis at the foot of each side with six butterflies above, separated by garlands of poppy-heads and wheat, with lilies at the top. Everything which Miss Sarah Losh designed by way of ornament was meant to be symbolical. So here we have presented to us at once one of the fundamental ideas of the Church - that of the resurrection, in the chrysalis and butterfly; and when the adornment of this window is viewed in combination with those on each side, we have what I take to be the other underlying thought of the whole Church - the infinite variety of modes in which the spirit of life exhibits itself. The window to the left shows forms of life connected with the sea - the fossil ammonites, the nautilus, seaweeds, and sea anemones. The window to the right shows things living in the air - the raven and the owl, the cockchafer and the bee, with branches of fir trees above bearing cones. In the centre we have the fruit and flowers of the earth. In the sea, on the earth, and in the air living things are found.

In a niche above the central window are two figures, representing St. Peter and St. Paul, the apostles of Jew and Gentile. Climbing up the gable end on each side is a series of nine small windows, each of which, when seen from the inside, will be found to exhibit, in stained glass, some different form of vegetation. The bell turret above, with a single bell, is surmounted by an eagle carved in stone. Projecting from the eaves at each side are grotesque reptilian figures. These serve no purpose as water-spouts, as they do in many old Cathedrals, but their ugly shapes are often explained to typify the flight of evil things from the holy place. One of these figures, however, the crocodile at the north-west corner, served a useful purpose. From his mouth smoke might once have been seen to issue. In the original heating system of the Church, a stove was placed below the floor in the centre of the nave, and a flue run beneath the surface diagonally to this corner, and up the wall through a chimney which terminated in the crocodile's mouth. This mode of heating was afterwards replaced by another, by means of hot air, the air being taken in through grids at the west end of the Church, passing along a trench to a furnace placed in the crypt, and thence back to the Church through grids at the eastern end. When this was done the turret-like chimney to the north-east was built. The same chimney serves now for the third mode of heating which has been adopted - that of low pressure hot water, distributed by pipes and radiators from a boiler placed in the crypt. The roof of the Church is of red Lazonby flags. The doorway of the crypt is that found built into the wall of the previous Chapel, to which reference has already been made.

Immediately to the right of the west door is a stone tank, surrounded by railings shaped as arrows. I have heard this described as an outside baptistry, but I think it more probable that Miss Losh meant it for a well, such as are sometimes found in connection with old churches. (She was evidently fond of wells. In addition to the "Katharine Well" on the Southwaite road, she renewed the stone basins of "St. Ninian's Well" at Brisco, and placed a canopy over one near Low Hurst.) A carved head with open mouth was apparently meant to deliver water, but none now flows through it, and the tank serves only to receive the drainage from the central walk.

On entering the Church we see that, simple as it is, and of no great size, it has a dignity of its own. Its proportions are good. The altar is well elevated, and stands forward from the eastern wall, having the apse as its background.

In the door are ingeniously contrived ventilators, with slides which can be opened or closed according to the weather. The lock is carved in the shape of two cones. Round the doorway is a carving in wood, representing a gourd plant, and at the base of the stem a caterpillar eating it off. This, no doubt, is an allusion to Jonah's gourd, and Dr. Lonsdale finds in its position here an emblem "of the Old Testament as a preparation for, or entrance into the New." The door opens upon a platform upon which to the left are the organ and the choir seats, and on the right the font, beyond which a corner has been screened off to form a small vestry. The font is a block of alabaster, carved in ten panels: a dove with olive leaf in its mouth reminds us both of our Lord's baptism and of the flood and ark, which are used as a type of baptism in the service; a dragonfly, which is hatched under water before beginning its flight in the air above; ears of corn; a butterfly; lilies; lotus flowers and leaves; a pine tree; pomegranate; melon; and vine with grapes. The cover of the font is silvered glass, to represent water, with lotus flowers and leaves upon it, carved in alabaster.

Three steps, between two pine cones on square pediments, lead down to the nave. The seats are of very substantial construction, the framework of oak, the panels and seats of Spanish chestnut. At the east of the nave three steps lead up to a platform of the same height as that at the west end, and on this are the lecterns, prayer-desk, and pulpit. Three further steps lead up to the apse, in the chord of which is placed the altar. There are two lecterns, very finely carved in chestnut wood; that to the north side is an eagle, with a Bible upon it; that to the south a pelican, bearing a Prayer Book. The pelican was often used as an emblem of our Lord, on account of the fable that it fed its young with blood from its own breast. Both birds are placed on pillars of black bog oak. The pulpit also is a single large trunk of bog oak. The wood, therefore, is probably more than a thousand years old, having grown to a large tree, and then been buried in a moss for centuries. It is roughly carved to represent a calamite - the kind of vegetation which grew upon the earth when the coal measures were being formed. By its side, to hold a candle, is a palm tree.

On either side is a large chair, also of black oak, but with an ebony panel as its back, beautifully carved, the one to the north showing the shepherds at the Nativity, and that to the south the wise men from the east bringing their gifts.

A bracket on the north wall is carved with a cock and an owl - birds of watchfulness, at morning and at evening.

At either side of the archway leading into the apse is a head, that of a man to the north and a woman to the south - the only human forms introduced into the structure of the Church, given here a place of honour, as belonging to the highest development of life upon earth. But up above, over the chancel arch, are seven angels, separated by palm trees, and an archangel at each side, one with a dragon carved on the bracket beneath his feet and the other with a bat pursuing a butterfly in the same position. The thought, no doubt, is that of the triumph of good over evil, the winged things of light trampling on the winged things of darkness, and their position there is to remind us that at every Eucharist of ours we join "with angels and archangels, and with all the company of heaven, to laud and magnify God's glorious name." The altar is a green marble slab supported by two bronze eagles. The eagle, here as in the bell turret and elsewhere, is an emblem of aspiration, and the Holy Table, borne on eagles' wings, is an invitation - "Sursum corda," "Lift up your hearts". On the stone pediment below are carved ears of corn and bunches of grapes, referring both to the elements of Holy Communion and to our Lord as the Bread of Life and true Vine. The altar candlesticks are of alabaster carved in the shape of lotus flowers. The lotus was a sacred emblem both in Egypt and India, its petals representing the rays of the sun, and its meaning, enlightenment; so here it is used to hold the two candles, which are types of our Lord as the Light of the World, in his two-fold nature of God and man.

Behind the centre of the sedilia which surround the apse is painted a lamb, as an emblem of Christ, with the sacred monogram below. Each of the other twelve is ornamented with the emblem of one of the twelve apostles, and below an Article of the Apostles' Creed. The sedilia are separated by stone pillars, each a single block of stone, standing free from the wall behind, with a capital carved with a design of its own. There is no repetition. Most show different forms of vegetation, but there are some animal forms introduced, among them an ibis devouring a toad. In the seven central niches the wall is pierced to receive lamps of different tints of orange colour. There are no wicks or oil in the lamps. The light is the daylight. Therefore I think that they form a more significant symbolism than the seven lamps which are frequently seen in churches abroad, and sometimes in England, suspended before the altar, to typify the seven gifts of the Spirit. These get their light each from its own oil and wick, but in the Wreay lamps the light comes from one and the same source, just as the One Spirit may exhibit itself in the form of different graces as it passes through different personalities. Above the sedilia is a semi-circular drum, with panels painted in fresco, showing chiefly passion flowers, lilies, and acanthus leaves. This drum is pierced by a row of small, deeply-set windows, twenty-nine in all, of plain glass, except the thirteen in the centre, which are filled with tracery. Thin sheets of alabaster have been carved to represent fossil forms, usually of ferns or other vegetation, but an insect in one case. A sheet of plain glass is placed outside the carving.

The two tall lampstands at either side of the sanctuary are made of metal, copied from those found at Pompeii, and lamps upon them are of the Roman shape. To attach the lamps to the stands Miss Losh gave the gold necklace chains of herself and her sister. These are now kept in the safe of the Church.

The Altar Service Book, like those on the lecterns, is bound in oak, with hinged back, the binding being as perfect to-day as it was when the Church was consecrated in 1842.

The roof of the nave is of fine solid openwork timber; each of the main transverse beams is carved with a different pattern, with a pendant cone from the centre.

The grouping of the windows is of interest. The symbolical numbers are three (for God), four (for creation), and seven (for completion or perfection). So at the west end of the Church there are three times three small windows at each side, climbing up to the apex of the roof, and three large windows below, making in all seven times three windows in that wall. At each side of the nave there are four windows, with a group of three above. All the windows in the Church, including the two small ones near the pulpit and the reading-desk, and those round the apse, number eighty-four, i.e., three, four, and seven multiplied together. All the windows, with the exception of those round the apse and the two by the pulpit and lectern, are filled with fragments of stained glass, leaded together without any regular pattern in most cases, though in some cases crosses or geometrical forms are introduced, and in each of the smaller ones a flower appears - a different one in each. These are shown in circles at the head of those windows in which the rest is filled with fragments; but in the case of the centre of each three in the nave walls, and each alternate window of those on the west gable, a thin sheet of stone has been carved in the shape of a flowering plant, and the interstices of the stone filled in with coloured glass. The only old glass is that used to form the "Deadly Nightshade" in the centre of the north-east group of three. This was formed of old French glass, picked up by Miss Losh's cousin, Mr. Losh, from among the ruins of the chapel of the palace of the Archbishop of Paris, when it had been wrecked by a mob. I suppose the special flower was chosen to typify the fatal effects of the revolutionary spirit when it is allowed to run riot.

Above the pulpit hangs an Italian lamp. A "scaldino" or chafing dish, also of Italian design, stands on the bracket near the reading desk, where also are figures of lions. The most interesting and valuable of the curios in the Church (kept now in the Church safe) is a bronze holy water pail, brought by Miss Losh from Normandy, probably of the 14th century, meant originally for asperging at funerals, having on its rim the inscription:

"PRIE PUR LALME G. GLANVILLE"

("Pray for the soul of G. Glanville").

Below are three castings of what appear to be figures of death - one blowing a horn and ringing a bell, a second as a reaper or grape-cutter, the third perhaps pouring out water from a vessel.

The present Church has been licensed for marriages since its consecration by Bishop Percy on December 1st, 1842, or very shortly afterwards. The marriage registers begin in August, 1844.

CHAPTER VIII: THE SCHOOL

THE early history of the School is intertwined with that of the Chapel. The same man was schoolmaster throughout the week and took the services in it on Sundays. In Lyson's Magna Britannica (Vol. 5, p.79), published in 1816, it is stated, "The school here was built about 1760, before which time the Chapel was used for that purpose." It was built upon Common Land, about twenty yards west of the Chapel yard. There was no conveyance of site or any trust-deed drawn up for it, nor for any of the other buildings which have followed it there. In spite of this absence of trust-deeds, the whole antecedents of the school made it easy to prove that it should be classed as a Church of England School at a Government Inquiry into the status of all Elementary Schools which followed upon the Education Act of 1902.

Miss Sarah Losh gives the following account of the building of the School which replaced that of 1760:- "The old Schoolhouse having become ruinous, my sister and I erected a new one, which was completed in 1830. The tything men had made over to us the old one that we might employ the materials in the work. We left the walls standing to serve for a court, and made use of the other materials on the spot, with the exception of some broken tables that were sold for 19 shillings by Mr. Robinson and Mr. Slack, who had obligingly consented to become trustees of the School, and who expended the amount in ale to refresh their neighbours, who very kindly made a boon day to smooth the green: a greater number having come than could have been expected, our supply of ale was exhausted, and we were sending for more when they anticipated. Mrs. M. Losh, as a token of goodwill, gave the School a stove and an oaken chair, which is curious, as being copied from one which had belonged to Glastonbury Abbey."

This old chair still survives in the present School, as do the east wall of Miss Losh's building (with the date of 1830 on it), and the north and south walls as far as the door on the south, before which a porch has since been built. Somewhere about the same time Miss Losh also built a "Dames' School," for infants, opposite Wreay Syke, and put a Mrs. Little in charge of it. This continued until after her death, for it is stated that the scholars of "both the Schools" took part in planting on the Green the memorial trees to her and her sister. But Mrs. Little had no successor as school-mistress there, and the infants were transferred to the School on the Green. An infant room was then built out as a wing to the north.

In 1874 Mr. William Septimus Losh, of Wreay Syke (a cousin of Miss S. Losh, and father of Mr. James Arlosh, of Woodside), added a Village Library, built in continuation of the infant room, with a connecting door between, as well as an entry from the Green.

The Library, however, has never been regarded an part of the School buildings. A small billiard table has now been placed in it for use by a "Wreay Men's Club," which meets there.

This infant room, at the last extensive alterations in the School, became the cloakroom and lavatory. A new infant room was built as a continuation of the main room, from which it is divided by a movable partition glazed in the upper part; the whole long room was reroofed; new outbuildings were also provided. These improvements were carried out between 1906 and 1910 at a cost of £713, towards which Mr. J. P. Fletcher's benefaction supplied £231, grants from the Diocesan Education Society and Betton's Charity £70, and the rest was raised by voluntary subscriptions, a sale of work, and other efforts.

As regards endowments the School brought away with it from its partnership with the Chapel the "stock" of about £40, which was adjudged to belong to it rather than to the Chapel. In 1763 Mr. John Brown, of Mellguards, left to it a legacy of £200. Of this sum £113 was laid out in the purchase of $7^{1}/2$ acres of copyhold land, the deed stating that the rent was to be used to increase the master's stipend. In 1778, by a Common Enclosure Award, a further 5 acres were assigned to "William Gaskin and his successors, Schoolmasters of Wreay for ever."

In 1838 Miss Sarah Losh let a field of about $1^{1}/2$ acres for 999 years, at a rent of "one peppercorn yearly, payable on the eleventh day of November, if the same shall be lawfully demanded," to Thomas Slack of Intack and John Robinson of Scalesceugh, and their successors, trustees of the said School. This was in lieu of the sum of £40, commonly called "Chapel Stock," then in her hands, and because she was "desirous of benefiting the School and raising the stipend of the schoolmaster." Upon one corner of this field she had built a cottage ("Pompeian Cottage") for the master's use. The rent of the field was to be used towards raising the stipend of the master, "or in such other manner as they or their successors (trustees of the said School) shall deem most for the benefit and advantage thereof."

At the same time Miss Losh let to the same trustees, for 999 years, at a peppercorn rent, another field of about 3 acres, in lieu of the sum of £87 in her hands, the balance of the legacy of Mr. John Brown, upon the same terms of trust. She also gave thirty acres of copyhold land to trustees for the Twelve Men, the rent of which was to be used for the payment of the school fees of children attending the School, but outside the chapelry. In 1867, after Miss Losh's death, a re-grant of this land was obtained from the Ecclesiastical Commissioners, as Lords of the Manor, to certain trustees for "The Ancient body known as the Twelve Men of Wreay, upon trust to permit the said Twelve Men to receive the rent and to expend the net profits thereof in or towards the Education, or for payment of School fees at the School of the Chapelry of Wreay, for such children of poor persons residing in the neighbourhood of the said Chapelry, but beyond the limits thereof, as they shall from time to time choose, nominate, or appoint at their usual accustomed time of meeting, as heretofore practised in the said Chapelry with regard to other matters connected with the same School of Wreay."

Having obtained the re-grant, the trustees then sold back the land to the owner of the Woodside Estate, and from the proceeds of the sale, £567 19s. 4d. Consols were purchased and vested in the Official Trustees of Charitable Funds. When school fees were abolished, the income from the trust was used by the managers towards the payment of the master and upkeep of the School. When, under the Education Act of 1902, the Local Education Authority became responsible for these expenses, the Board of Education held an inquiry into the origin of all endowments connected with Elementary Schools. In this case they decided that it was not one originally intended for the payment of the master or upkeep of the School, but for the benefit of children attending it. Accordingly they granted a scheme for its management in January, 1906. Under this scheme it is to be known as "The Losh Foundation," and managed by twelve ex-officio trustees, the Twelve Men of Wreay, and one representative trustee appointed by the County Council of Cumberland. A very wide discretion is left with the trustees in the use of the funds. Exhibitions may be given to children leaving the School to go to a Secondary School, books may be bought for the School Library, facilities may be provided for gardening, gymnastic training, cookery, laundry work, dairy work, or handicraft; they are also empowered to receive additional donations or endowments for the same purposes. The annual interest on the Consols amounts to £14 4s. 0d., but as £150 of accumulated income has been invested in 5 per cent. War Loan, the present income of the Foundation amounts to £21 14s. 0d.

In 1858 Mr. J. P. Fletcher gave £200 Maryport and Carlisle Debenture Stock for "educating the children of the poor living in and around Wreay, but particularly "those in the vicinity of Wreay Hall." At the time of the inquiry into school endowments after the 1902 Act, Mr. Fletcher was still living, and with his consent, and that of the Board of Education, the whole capital, resulting from the sale of the Stock, with unexpended income, amounting in all to £231 15s. 9d., was allowed to be used towards the School improvements then made.

As the result of the same inquiry the Board decided that the rent of the field bought with the £40 ancient "Chapel Stock," upon which Miss Losh had built a master's house, should be paid to the managers towards the expenses for which they were liable, but that the rents of all those fields purchased by the bequest of Mr. John Brown, and augmented by the Common Enclosure Award, ought to be paid over by the trustees to the Local Education Authority, and used by that Authority for the relief of the rates of the parishes which were served by the School. The Twelve Men, however, were very loath to pay over, for the relief of rates, the proceeds of an endowment which was evidently meant for the educational benefit of Wreay and the neighbourhood. Accordingly, whilst the rent of the master's house and adjoining field was paid over each year to the School Managers' Account, the net income from the other land was left to accumulate in the bank, or invested in Government Stock, in the hope that further legislation would permit a different use to be made of it. By the Education Act of 1921 a wider discretion was left in the hands of the Board of Education, and in 1926 that Board granted a scheme, with the consent of the civil Parish Meeting and the Local Education Authority, for the future use of the income arising therefrom. They made it a condition, however, that the whole of the accumulations of past rents should be paid over to the Local Education Authority, in accordance with their first decision. The accumulations amounted to £50, and this was divided by the Local Education Authority in the proportion of two fifths to the parish rates of Wreay, two-fifths to Hesket-in-the-Forest, and one-fifth to St. Cuthbert Without.

The land was then sold to A. Gibson, Esq., J.P., of Woodside, and with the purchase price, £744 17s. 2d. 5 per cent. War Loan Stock was purchased, producing an annual income of £37 4s. 10d.

Under the scheme the trust is to be known as the "School Lands Educational Foundation." Its management is to be in the hands of the same trustees as the Losh Foundation. Three pounds a year are to be paid to the managers of the School towards the upkeep of the buildings so long as it remains a Voluntary School. The rest of the income may be used in assisting pupils to attend schools or classes for secondary education, making arrangements for attending to the health of the children in the School, or "otherwise promoting the education, including social and physical training, of boys and girls of the poorer classes in the said Chapelry." It will be seen that the last provision gives to the trustees even a wider discretion than they have under the Losh Scheme. Under it they have arranged visits by the elder scholars to the Cathedral, the Bird Room at Tullie House, and Messrs. Ferguson's, Holme Head Works, and intend to send them from time to time to other places of historical interest and industrial works.

The School buildings will now compare favourably with those of any other village in the county. They serve not only as a place for teaching children, but also as the centre of the social life of the parish; lectures and concerts are given there. Evening classes are held for such subjects as sewing, cookery, nursing, dairy work, folk-dancing, and singing. The members of the Men's Club use the Library, with its billiard table, almost every night in the winter months, and frequently overflow into the adjoining room, which is put at their disposal for cards and other games. Here the Women's Institute have their monthly meetings, which always include a tea, whatever the rest of the evening's occupation may be. Whist drives and dances are held from time to time for the benefit of one organization or another.

For the children, also, the School is more than the place where they learn their lessons: it is their home for the day. Very few of them live near enough to go back for dinner, the great majority bringing their food with them, and living in the School or on the Green from morning till evening; they keep the School rooms bright with flowers most of the year. There is a complete development of monitors' duties - some are responsible for sweeping up the hearths, some for mending the fires, when necessary; some lighting the fire in the large cloakroom, in preparation for the mid-day meal; some for making the tea; some for giving out the books and stationery; some for looking after the piano and music; some for helping to keep the books of the School Savings Bank. A list of those responsible for these and other duties is posted up in the School. The School Bank, affiliated to the Carlisle and County Savings Bank, is used both by past scholars and future scholars, as well as by those actually attending the School. In some cases the mother opens an account for a child as soon as it is born.

The Village Green is a valuable adjunct to the School buildings. On summer days a class may sometimes be seen upon it, receiving their instruction and enjoying a sun-bath at the same time, or under the shade of the trees if the rays of the sun prove too strong. Almost every day, summer and winter, when it does not rain, for a certain time each morning the scholars are there playing their "organized games," or drilling on the paved parts immediately surrounding the School.

The list of masters up to Mr. Gaskin coincides with that of the readers or curates of the Chapel.

Mr. Gaskin did not hold the mastership up to his death, for whilst he was still incumbent the name of Mr. Noble appears as schoolmaster; he probably held the post until about 1850, and was succeeded by Mr. B. Olivant until 1862. Then Mr. W. Postlethwaite became master; he brought up a large family at Wreay, and after holding the mastership for thirty years he went out to South Africa, but soon returned, and became master of a small village school near Kirkby Stephen in Westmorland. Mr. H. B. Bancks followed him in 1892 until 1904, when he left to be master of Fladbury School, in Worcestershire. After him Mr. C. Homer held the mastership for five years, and Mr. R. Udall for three years. The latter emigrated to East Africa, and is now settled at Ruiru, near Nairobi. His successor, in 1913, was the present master, Mr. R. Jardine.

In 1905 a wash-house and other outbuildings were added to the master's house, and improvements made inside, at a cost of £88. In 1928 the whole of the interior was re-arranged, and a new kitchen added, at a cost of £122.

The number of children attending the School is usually between 60 and 70. The salary of the headmastership, under the county scale, is from a minimum of £180 (in the unlikely event of a headmaster being appointed immediately after taking his certificate) to a maximum of £360.

CHAPTER IX: THE CHURCHYARD & CEMETERY

The post-Reformation Chapel at Wreay appears to have been built on Common land, but burials began to take place there in 1750, so there must then have been an enclosed space around it. This forms the greater part of the present burial yard to the north of the present Church. After Wreay Common was enclosed in 1778, the Twelve Men gave permission to the Clerk to fence off a further piece of ground, as a pasture for his cow, entirely surrounding the graveyard. The roadway then ran in a straight course down Chapel Hill, passing north of the Church, coming out on to the Carlisle road opposite Wreay Syke.

In exchange for this land, in 1836, Miss Losh gave another field for the Clerk, adjoining that in which she had built a house for the schoolmaster. She then got permission to divert the road along its present course to the west and south of the Clerk's old enclosure, of which she used that portion which lay between the old graveyard and the new roadway to the south, as a site for the new Church, with its surrounding grass terraces. The strip between the graveyard and old road to the north she gave for consecration as additional ground for burials. In a plot in the north-east corner, adjoining the Losh burial ground, but outside the Churchyard, she placed the memorial cross to her parents, the cenotaph to her sister, and the tree planted in memory of Major Thain; the rest of the land she planted with trees and shrubs.

The field acquired in 1836 was sold in 1926, and the amount, invested in 5 per cent. War Loan Stock, now produces an annual income of £14 17s. l0d. for the Clerk.

Among the gravestones is one carved in the shape of a tree trunk, in memory of John Smallwood, who was killed by the fall of tree which was being felled for use in the building of the Church. Another, a rough block of stone, records the death of a workman by a fall of rock in a quarry.

Miss Losh also conveyed to the Dean and Chapter of Carlisle, as rectors of the parish and patrons of the benefice, an acre of ground which she had laid out as a cemetery, the deed providing that fees for all vaults, graves, tombstones, and burials should be paid to the incumbent of Wreay for the time being. It was consecrated by the Bishop of Carlisle on May 12th, 1842; thus it became, to all intents and purposes, an extension of the Church burial ground, though it is situated about a quarter of a mile from the Church. It lies to the west of the Carlisle road, but is quite invisible from that or any other public road, being entirely surrounded by plantations of trees. Peaceful seclusion from the world was evidently what Miss Losh hoped to secure by this selection of the site, and she achieved her object. From the Carlisle road a short lane, between trees, leads past the Chapel, which is also kept invisible from the road by a turn in the lane, up to the Cemetery gates.

A few years earlier, in 1835, there had been excavated from the sand dunes of the north-west coast of Cornwall what may have been the oldest surviving place of Christian worship in England, the Chapel of St. Piran or Perran. St. Piran had come from Ireland to preach the Gospel in Cornwall; his most probable date was about 600 A.D. In after days he was much reverenced, and relics of him were preserved in Exeter Cathedral, and elsewhere; he was reckoned the patron Saint of the tin miners. Whether or not the Chapel of Perran-zabulo (i.e., in zabulo, "in the sand") dates from the time of the Saint, the rough style of its masonry is consistent with its having been built in very early times. It owes its preservation to the sands, which had filled and covered it. Its fate was not unlike that of Pompeii, though due to the action of the north west winds instead of a volcano. As soon as its walls were uncovered, they quickly began to fall into ruin, so that now there is not much to be seen above ground except one gable end, and the remains of the other walls, a few feet high, and an altar-tomb.

Miss Losh reproduced, as far as she could, this ancient oratory as her Cemetery Chapel. The plan is the same - a simple rectangle. The dimensions are the same - 29 feet long, $16^{1}/_{2}$ feet broad, and walls 13 feet high. The stone altar, or altar-tomb, is copied from that at Perranzabulo, so also one of the doorways, with the three carved heads, but the doors are of greater breadth, as also the windows, with the exception of the narrow window in the south wall. In Cornwall the roof had entirely gone; the Wreay Chapel roof is of sandstone flags externally, and a barrel-vault of plaster internally.

Miss Losh also built a cottage for the sexton, adjoining the lane into the Cemetery.

The Cemetery was not much used by the people of Wreay for many years. They naturally preferred to lay their friends in the extension of the old burial yard, which was made in the same year. Out of 28 burials in the Cemetery during the first 25 years after consecration, only six were from the present parish of Wreay, with its extended boundaries, and the rest came from outside, 14 of them from Carlisle, but as the small addition to the old yard became more filled, much fuller use was made of the Cemetery, and now the great majority of burials takes place there. There have been in all 286 burials in it, and as it is estimated that there remain yet about 800 vacant grave-spaces, it is likely to suffice for the needs of the parish for many generations to come.

A Survey of the Literature on the Church and Sarah Losh

The entry in "Mannix and Whellan's Directory" from 1847 offers a brief description of St. Mary's Church, which is worth giving in full as it represents an unopinionated response and was published shortly after Sarah Losh's death:

"The chapel was entirely rebuilt in 1843, at a cost of about £1,200; the whole of which sum, with the exception of a small donation from the patrons of the living, and the contributions of a few friends, was defrayed by Miss Losh, of Woodside. It is in the Norman style, consisting of nave and chancel, with turret, crowned by a Roman eagle, and containing, in two niches, statues of Saints Peter and Paul. The western doorway, which is arched, is much admired, being ornamented with flowers of the water lily, &c. The interior is very neat, and all the windows being of stained glass, the "dim religious light," adds much to the impressiveness and solemnity of the sacred edifice; the three in the west end are richly executed. The chancel, which is semi-circular in form, is very beautiful, and its windows are cut to represent antediluvian flowers. Here are seven lamps, apparently lighted, intended to represent the seven spirits mentioned in the Book of Revelations. Two eagles in brass support the communion table; another, richly carved in wood, serves as a reading desk; and numerous figures of angels, birds, &-c. ornament the interior of the structure. The oaken roof of the chapel is also beautifully carved, and was furnished from the well wooded lawn of Woodside, the seat of Miss Losh, whose prolific mind furnished the various devices for this splendid little edifice, which is fitted up in the style of some of the Italian churches. In the adjoining churchyard, there is a beautiful monument, by Dunbar, to the memory of the late Miss Catherine Losh. It consists of a figure of the deceased in white polished marble, and occupies an antique Druidical cell, near to which stands a stone cross, eighteen feet high, a copy of one in Bewcastle churchyard, with a Latin inscription to the memory of the late John Losh, Esq. and his wife. The cemetery at a short distance from the chapel, as also the sexton's house, was the gift of Miss Losh. The former contains a neat oratory, a copy of one at Perranzabuloe, Cornwall."

It is interesting that there is no criticism or even a sense of the buildings uniqueness, but simply a resort to general terms of approbation: "much admired", "neat", "dim religious light", "impressiveness and solemnity", "very beautiful" etc. There is a specific reference to the seven lamps representing the seven spirits from Revelations.

Later directories - and they were published on a regular basis - following the practice of the time, copied or paraphrased the "Mannix and Whellan" description.

Dante Gabriel Rossetti, poet and painter, was a friend of Sarah's cousin, Margaret Alicia Losh and was her guest for two nights at Ravenside in 1869. On Saturday, 21st August, when he had journeyed on to Penkill Castle in Ayrshire, the home of Sarah's cousin, Margaret, daughter of William Losh, he wrote with energetic enthusiasm to his mother. He addressed her with his customary filial salutation: "Good Antique,

Here I am since Thursday afternoon, as I know you will be glad to hear in your maternal solicitude. I left London on Tuesday, and spent two nights and a day at old Miss Losh's house near Carlisle, where, as you may be sure, she made me very comfortable. I saw in the neighbourhood some most remarkable architectural works by a former Miss Losh, who was the head of the family about the year 1830. She must have been really a great genius, and should be better known. She built a church in the Byzantine style, which is full of beauty and imaginative detail, though extremely severe and simple. Also a mausoleum to her sister - a curious kind of Egyptian pile of stones with a statue of the lady in the centre, and opposite a Saxon cross - a sort of obelisk, reproduced from an old one, but with restorations by the lady herself. Also a Pompeian house for the schoolmaster, a parsonage, and a most interesting cemetery-chapel attached to a cemetery which she presented to the parish before such things were instituted by law. The chapel is an exact reproduction of one which was found buried in the sands in Cornwall, and excited a good deal of controversy at the time under the name of `The Lost Church!' She also built a large addition to the family mansion at Woodside in the Tudor style. All these things are real works of genius, but especially the church at Wreay, a most beautiful thing. She was entirely without systematic study as an architect, but her practical as well as inventive powers were extraordinary. I am sure the whole of this group of her works would interest you extremely, and I should suggest your paying a visit to the neighbourhood on one of your holidays. There is also most lovely scenery, and some amiable Loshes besides the Miss Losh you wot of, whose house is called Ravenside (five miles from Carlisle), where I am sure she would be delighted to welcome you and yours if she heard you were likely to come her way. I suppose you would not be able to go this year, or it is possible I may be in the neighbourhood again on my way back to London. However, my movements are rather uncertain at present as to time, as I am not sure how long I may be able to remain here, from various causes."

He also wrote with equal enthusiasm to Janey Morris: "I have been here since last Thursday, having spent a day on the road at old Miss Losh's house near Carlisle. The neighbourhood there is a beautiful one, and there are some really extraordinary architectural works - a church of a byzantine style and other things - erected from her own designs by a lady of Miss Losh's family who has been dead some years and who must certainly have been a true genius. The works are very original and beautiful, very much more so than the things done by the young architects now, and they were done as far back as 1830 without any professional assistance or directed study, though the practical part of them is quite as remarkable as the invention. I was very much interested and should like Webb to see them. The place is called Wreay."

It is very probable that Philip Webb did get to see Wreay. He was a friend of George Howard, later Earl of Carlisle, who lived 12 miles to the east of Carlisle, at Naworth Castle. He commissioned Webb to build two houses for him in Brampton. In 1878, Philip Webb built his only church, St. Martin's, in Brampton.

Rossetti's enthusiasm is evident, but his comments also reveal the views of Sarah Losh's niece, Alicia, especially the point that the "cemetery-chapel" was felt to be an "exact reproduction" and the cross "reproduced from an old one, but with restorations by the lady herself". He also corroborates the use of the word Byzantine and, perhaps, indicates a family tradition of Egyptian and Pompeian inspiration for the works. Incidentally, Rossetti's use of the word "pompeian" here is quoted as an early illustration of the word's use in 'The Oxford English Dictionary'. His point that the buildings were done "without any professional assistance or directed study, though the practical part of them is quite as remarkable as the invention" is a clear statement, with a degree of authority, for Sarah Losh being the sole author of the works.

Rossetti's friend, William Bell Scott in his "Autobiographies" was equally attracted by the "Byzantine chapel at Wreay", but he was somewhat patronising in his approval. He observed a "taste and power of intelligent design altogether unusual among women" and felt that Sarah Losh was "entitled to a place in artistic dictionaries".

Dr Henry Lonsdale published his account of Sara Losh and the church in 1873. In his general preface he says: "Miss Sara Losh of Woodside ranked with the highest intellectual class, and displayed a marvellous aptitude for art and architectural design, as well as various branches of science; her knowledge of ancient and modern languages was no les noted and special."

Lonsdale's interpretation of the church must be taken very seriously. His account begins with an apparently unquestioning reliance on Walcott's 'Archaeology', but but he appends a footnote which is revealing: "Walcott's 'Sacred Archaeology' is the authority for these explanations. It is well to note, however, that the emblems mentioned above are differently construed by different authorities, and that ecclesiologists are more disposed to assign a Christian meaning than to consider the mythological element so largely prevailing historically. The able and recondite work of my friend, Mr. Thomas Inman of Liverpool, entitled 'Ancient Faiths embodied in Ancient Names,' has opened out a vein of curious speculation that behoves the attention of those searching for larger interpretation of these emblems". Inman, like Lonsdale, was a distinguished medical man, who made mythography his hobby. The "Dictionary of National Biography" sums his mythographic work up concisely: "He had little original scholarship, but read widely, and, although the philological basis of his researches is quite unscientific, his writings display great ingenuity." He saw phallic worship as the key to all mythology.

Lonsdale makes many challenging statements: "Miss Losh's insight into the past is marked by largeness of view, and a spacious conception of human worship through its initiatory stages of fetishisms, mystic longings and superstitions, onward to the more modern interpretation that seeks solace in churches and an ordained priesthood". "There is unity of purpose throughout the work, showing the development of the different Cults, from the time of Osiris and his Nilotic nymphs, through the days of the wise King, bright in his polygamy and home virtues, down to the monogamic non-virtuous Anglo-Saxon, accredited with representing the latest phase of civilization!"

Between the lines the erudite doctor may even be delighting in thinking that Sara Losh has hoodwinked the Bishop and other authorities by making the church emblematic of all religions. His case is that here is a Christian Church that in embodying (some of) the mysteries of the Christian faith also portrays man's historical impulse to religion. He makes no mention of the extent to which the imagery - the cones and the arrows, for example, - might be partly personal.

The problem is to determine the basis of Lonsdale's authority and the extent to which these views might have been in Sara Losh's mind when she built the church.

Victorian and Edwardian guides to the county - and they are to be found in abundance - make no reference to the church. It was, perhaps too out of the way, aesthetically and geographically, and too modern, to excite their curiosity.

The first subjective discussion of the church in print, other than that by Lonsdale, is by a Carlisle man, George Topping, who wrote a series of well-informed, genial essays called "Rambles in the Borderland with the Clan" (1921). After an entertaining account of the Losh family history - he recalls locals commenting on the Dundonald/Losh experiments - "sum uncanny work o' sum kein was bein' carried on - magic or witchcraft, or sum devil's work o' that sort" - he turns to the church. The church, he says, "will serve to perpetuate for many years to come the exquisite taste and refinement of this highly-accomplished mistress of Woodside". Topping recognizes the Roman basilica form, senses "a cathedral-like tone" and finds that, "Symbolic teaching is everywhere". The gourd, the seven lamps, the two eagles each have their meaning and, when he looks at the font he sees, "Its lines suggesting purity, its butterflies transition to a new life, and its scheme as a whole the 'ineffable union betwixt Christ and His Church, and hope in immortality' ". The Clan view the Mausoleum and the Cross appreciatively and then "doff their caps to the memory of a great and good woman". Topping's view of the church is probably fairly representative of that held by local people at the time.

Canon Hall was the priest in charge at Wreay for forty seven years from 1893 to 1940. He published a short history of the village in1929 towards the end of his ministry. He can claim a far more intimate and extended knowledge of the church and the parish than anyone else, including Lonsdale, who has written about St. Mary's. He would be aware of oral memories within the parish concerning Sara Losh and would be the recipient of any tradition of interpretation that persisted. Sara Losh was alive for over a decade after the church had been built and it is not unreasonable to suppose that she would have offered some explanation of the imagery to her priest at the time, the Rev. Richard Jackson, and to other parishioners.

In "Wreay" Canon Hall offers an extended and itemised interpretation of the church. He insists, without justification, that: "Everything which Miss Sarah Losh designed by way of ornament was meant to be symbolical". He then chooses to read the church almost as an orthodox parable, again offering no justification, and only in the most obvious cases referring to any symbolic tradition. There seems a readiness on his part to provide a facile and unquestioning explanation of the imagery. His approach is well displayed when he discusses the carving on the windows on the West Front. Looking at the centre window with "a chrysalis at the foot of each side with six butterflies above, separated by garlands of poppy-heads and wheat, with lilies at the top", he explains: "So here we have presented to us at once one of the fundamental ideas of the Church - that of the resurrection, in the chrysalis and butterfly; and when the adornment of this window is viewed in combination with those on each side, we have what I take to be the other underlying thought of the whole Church - the infinite variety of modes in which the spirit of life exhibits itself". His understanding is sensitive and sympathetic, but there is no reason to think that it coincides with the intentions of an independent-minded Sara Losh.

Hall also has a good sense of the practical woman, understanding the problems of building in a wet area and the work that needed to be undertaken, and he recalls the memories still alive in the village of the old lady in her black bonnet walking from Woodside into the village.

Arthur Mee's "King's England" series of county books must have been one of the most successful of all topographical publishing ventures. Mee relied heavily on local informants, many from the clergy, to provide detailed coverage of village churches, monuments and anecdotes. "The Lake Counties" allocates generous space to St. Mary's, is attracted by the personal elements of the story, the sisterly devotion, but is not drawn into suggesting a romantic attachment to William Thain. Mee emphasizes the individuality of the work. He sees the church as "a striking place packed with symbolism, with fine craftsmanship, and with curious and unusual things", but his account proceeds to enthusiastically list the curious things and describe the craftsmanship rather than to elaborate the symbolism. The font he finds "perhaps too elaborately" carved, but otherwise he is entranced with the detail of the church: "We must all appreciate the ingenuity and the loving labour put into this remarkable place, as well as the fine craftsmanship".

Mee credits "three artists, the lady of Woodside, the local mason, and John Scott the cripple". He does tell one new anecdote: "It was characteristic of Sarah Losh, who did all this work for love, that she should wish no name to appear anywhere on the church; it was to be a work of faith and love with no self praise in it, and not a single name or mark of recognition was to appear. . . . One day it was necessary to remove the font, and as the bowl was lifted from the shaft a well-kept secret was revealed. It was the man and not the woman who could not keep a secret, for on the bottom of the bowl, where he thought it never would be seen, the proud mason had slyly carved his name".

Nikolaus Pevsner's account in "The Buildings of England: Cumberland and Westmorland" (1967) is magisterially concise and erudite. He finds St. Mary's "a crazy building without any doubt, even if it is a most impressive and in some ways amazingly forward-pointing building". He argues for the building's historical uniqueness. Its Lombardic style, and it is more Lombardic than Byzantine or Norman, is contemporary with other English examples. The churches at Wilton. Streatham and Watney Street had been anticipated by German designs, but it is improbable that Sara Losh was aware of these precedents. Her positioning of the altar, with the priest facing the congregation, is almost certainly borrowed from Early Christian practice, and would be almost unique at the time, and much of the carving and workmanship anticipates the Arts and Crafts Movement by half a century. He finds "the whole church and the furnishings are replete with symbolism", although he does not develop the significance of the symbols any further. He understands the church as "reminiscent of (Sarah's) travels (with Katharine) and beautified by symbolic conceits", which suggests that the symbols are to be read in a personal way.

Pevsner clarifies the eclectic mix of styles: "the Italian Romanesque of the gallery in the west end and the French Romanesque of the columns in the apse and the absence of aisles, and much else, the clerestory windows, for example, which belongs to no style". "In short, Miss Losh is quite free in her interpretation, and quite original."

The rest of his account is a crisp enumeration of the church's features and decoration. He points out that her use of decoration is "as remarkable as her architectural choices" and insists that the cross, with its ornamental, more realistic, carving is not simply a copy of the Bewcastle Cross.

Nikolaus's Pevsner's article in "The Architectural Review" repeats his description in the "Buildings of England".

Norman Nicholson, ("Greater Lakeland", 1969), the fine poet and county topographer from Millom, was sceptical of Pevsner's enthusiasm. For him the church is a "freak" and a "fascinating ecclesiastical folly". He is out of sympathy with the building: "window surrounds crawling with butterflies and beetles"; "Inside , the effect is even odder"; "the raised sanctuary looks for all the world like the setting of an Italian opera": an altar "more suited to a pagan temple". He represents the "love" of Sara for William Thain as established fact, and suggests the arrow in the wall is "as if the choirboys had been playing Robin Hood". He sees the "tropical images - the crocodiles and snakes on the roof, and, above all, the otherwise preposterous palm tree" as only making sense as part of a romantic memorial to a soldier killed in the tropics. It is a strangely dismissive and superficial view from a normally sensitive observer, one who knew the church well. It represents the extreme version of those who would see St. Mary's as the product of caprice.

St Mary's next appeared as "one of the most peculiar village churches in England" in a pleasant, business-like article by M.A..Woods in Country Life magazine in November, 1971. Woods tells the story of the Losh sisters and their family in an easy generalising way - she suggests Katharine might have been engaged to William Thain - and provides a practical description of the church. She suggests that Sara had ready access through family connections to continental developments (a careless reading of Pevsner) and presents a non-committal view on the significance of the work: "Sara freely borrowed designs and symbolism from all faiths and adapted them to illustrate Christian beliefs, especially those revealed through nature." Such an article, however, was bringing the church to the attention of a far wider audience.

Marshall Hall's "Dictionary of Cumbrian Artists" provides short entries for Sarah Losh, William Hindson, John Scott, David Dunbar and William Septimus Losh. His sources are Lonsdale, Arthur Mee and Pevsner.

The longest account of the church to date is an B.Arch. dissertation by Katharine Drew for Newcastle University. She takes all of Pevsner's points and expands on them usefully and brings together such information as there is in other documentation. She introduces the name of Thomas Hope and gives examples of his illustrations of Lombardic churches at Pavia, Ancona and Spoleto which were published in 1835 and must have been available to Sara Losh. She also suggests that the Norman Church at Kilpeck in Herefordshire with its rich animal imagery and the Norman/Danish font at Bridekirk, Cockermouth, which is carved with animals, may have been influential. The imagery and symbolism in the church is somewhat naively ascribed to pantheism: "Only such a pantheistic belief could reconcile the presence of such thoroughly Christian symbols as the caterpillar-chrysalis-butterfly theme of Resurrection with that of the antediluvian fern and fossil representations which Lonsdale suggests are an 'acknowledgement to nature-worship; or the first idealistic breathings towards the infinite and the unknown' ".

Laurie Kemp, who has lived in Wreay for many years, wrote an entertaining account of the Loshes and people associated with Woodside over the years, but, apart from a chapter on Sarah Losh, which largely dramatises some anecdotes from Lonsdale's account, he does not develop any views on the church or her work.

John Martin Robinson, in his survey of English buildings in 1986, finds St. Mary's "unique", "an extraordinary apparition" with "mind-blowing church furnishings". The graves are "odd and personal". He sees the personal inspiration of the work: "The architecture of the church shows a remarkable range of sources, illustrating the breadth of Sara's learning and intended to recall her and her sister's travels together". He sees the decoration as symbolic without developing the idea, and finds William Hindson's sculpture "weird". The carvings are "like specimens in a Victorian album", and the gargoyles are, "Even odder, but equally enjoyable".

Simon Jenkins, the "Times" journalist, in his 'England's Thousand Best Churches" awards St. Mary's four stars and gives it the accolade of being in the top hundred churches. He does this despite, or because of its being, "one of the most eccentric small churches in England". He sees the "caterpillar, chrysalis and butterfly as symbols of life, death and resurrection and finds the stained glass "lovely", but the furnishings are, oddly, "Disneyesque, except that they are stylistically harmonious and superbly executed". Jenkins's description is efficient and enthusiastic and he employs some resonating if loose terms to describe the church and its architect: "Sara Losh's Cumbrian homage to love"; "Sara Losh was an individual genius, a Charlotte Bronte of wood and stone". His enthusiasm and the success of the book have served to bring the church to the notice of a wider public.

Rosemary Hill, writing in "Crafts Magazine, 2000", is another enthusiast possessed of a good phrase: "She had all the innocent daring of the autodidact" but she does insist that, "Sara Losh is not naive or thoughtless in what she did". Her attitude to handwork anticipates that of Ruskin: "As an example of craft and architecture in harmony and of their value as a unifying moral and social force, St. Mary's, Wreay, was a vastly greater success than the Oxford Museum", the building in which Ruskin and his ideas played the greatest active role, which was begun fifteen years later.

Rosemary Hill recognizes Sara Losh's originality and determined individuality, and has time to look closely at the windows: "Indeed the windows were made by William Wailes of Newcastle, one of the best known stained glass artists of the day. Wailes was working at the same time for Pugin. Losh must have been quite as decided as Pugin himself in her ideas, for Wailes never made anything else like the scheme at Wreay".

For Hill, "Much of the symbolism is not Christian at all but pagan or personal", but she doesn't elaborate further on either its significance or its origin. She does accord Sara Losh the highest respect as an artist: "If artistic value is to be measured by an ability to seize the currents of thought and feeling that run through the age and give them fresh and vital expression, Sara Losh and her church are very important indeed".

Sara Losh has received an entry in the latest edition of "The Oxford Dictionary of National Biography". Previously only her uncle, James Losh, had been so honoured. The concise account by Charles Plouviez draws on Rosemary Hill's words on Sara Losh's "artistic value" quoted immediately above. Plouviez feels that, "The finished building has a total coherence and affecting simplicity". He speaks of the "prolific, vigorously expressive decoration", and suggests that: "The profusion of naturalistic ornament is best explained as an attempt to express a pantheistic celebration of creation". He emphasises that: "There is no distinctive Christian symbolism, not even a cross, but the vitality of the carvings and the use of natural forms reflects the cycle of death, rebirth, and eternity".

Writing in "The Guardian", (6/8/2005) Jane Stevenson presents Sara Losh as a Romantic, feminist icon. Stevenson makes bold, unsubstantiated statements, such as, "She refused to marry in case it compromised her independence", but she does make a vigorous case for the individuality and originality of the work. "With utter self-confidence, she manipulated aspects of the Christian heritage which were alien to the Anglican tradition, and at the same time, deployed a completely idiosyncratic symbolic vocabulary". Again the argument is made for Sarah Losh as a precursor of the Arts and Crafts Movement: "By a wonderful irony, one of the greatest of all Ruskinian buildings pre-dated the Ruskinian revolution by a decade, and was built by a woman".

An unexpected view of Sara Losh is to be found in an unsigned article in "Geology Today", January 2005. It suggests links between some of the imagery in the church and newly discovered fossils in the carboniferous measures in the North-east that were exciting the interest of members of the Literary and Philosophical Society in Newcastle. We would expect Sarah Losh to be aware of such developments. Her father had been an enthusiast for fossils, her uncle was actively involved in the coal industry, and she had a substantial commercial interest as well as a keen scientific curiosity. We are told that the bog oak pulpit has the external markings of a calamites; the "palm tree" on the grave slab looks suspiciously like a Lepidodendron complete with a distinctive stigmarian root spread and the "gargoyles" on the corbels are "in fact contemporary reconstructions of Megalosaurus and Dicynodon". The Wreay images preceded the first formal scientific description of them by months. The author would add Sara Losh to "the impressive list of women who contributed to the golden age of geology as a new science, for whom the works of the Lord did not exclude the wonders of the fossil record".

The most considered account of the church is by Barrie Bullen, Professor of English at Reading University. It was published in the Burlington Magazine in July, 2005, and also presented as part of the extended discussion in his book, "Continental Crosscurrents: British Criticism and European Art 1810-1910".

He speculates on and makes a convincing argument for Losh using Thomas Hope's "History of Architecture" and making reference to various books on symbolism and mythology.

Perhaps, more controversially, he establishes parallels between her use of imagery and the arguments put forward by the pantheistic Richard Payne Wright. Payne Wright published a book, "Two Essays on the Worship of Priapus" in the year Sarah Losh was born.

It is worth quoting Bullen's comments at length, because they are at the heart of his argument and represent a strong statement of the case for reading the church's symbolism in a non-orthodox-Christian way: "The style and decoration of St. Mary's suggest that Sara Losh was well aware of the rituals of the early Church and the growing controversies around church design. "One of the current issues involved the mythographic connexion between ancient religions and Christianity". Bullen quotes an anonymous reviewer from 1829: "Philosophy, religion, history and poetry, are the component parts of mythology, the knowledge of the universal language of nature, as expressed by certain symbols". This view certainly suggests the complex way we should be prepared to understand St. Mary's.

Bullen argues that Payne Knight's "An Inquiry into the Symbolical Language of Ancient Art and Mythology" (1818) is of key relevance: "reissued in 1836, at precisely the moment when Losh must have been contemplating the design of St. Mary's, and almost every one of the symbols that she uses in the decoration of her church has a place in his work. The guardians of the chapel are all there - the snake ('symbols of health and immortality'), the tortoise ('immortality'), and the eagle ('creation, preservation, and destruction'). The caterpillar, chrysalis and butterfly, all of which appear on the windows of the west front, are related by Payne Knight to 'an emblem of man in his earthly form', 'a natural image of death' and|'the celestial or ethereal soul' ". In other words, they are representative of the passage from birth, life, through death to immortality." . . .SaraH Losh may have been less sceptical in her view of Christianity, but St. Mary's is filled with imagery that suggests the continuity of religious belief and the recognition that much pagan symbolism had been taken up by Christianity.

"The majority of Losh's chosen forms both outside and inside the church are connected with fertility, the generation of life, and the male and female principles. The lotus flower, the pomegranate and the barley corn, emblems distributed throughout the church, are representative, says Payne Knight, of `the passive generative power' of the female, while a ubiquitous motif at St. Mary's is the pine- or fir-cone, identified by him with phallic mysteries and as fundamental to many religious beliefs". . . . And, most significantly, Bullen suggests, the motif also occurs in the mausoleum dedicated to Katharine Losh, whose classically posed figure is shown in rapt contemplation of a fir-cone. The idea that the serene Katharine is contemplating a phallic image would seem to tax the most enthusiastic mythographer's imagination.

"As Payne Knight points out, the pine-cone appears on the end of Bacchus's thyrsus and `therefore holds the place of the male, or active generative attribute'." "But, as Sara Losh well knew, the pine-cone had been adopted by Christianity as a symbol of resurrection and immortality. When she was in Rome . . . where she would have seen the colossal pine-cone forming part of the fountain in the Cortile della Pigna. Three and a half metres high, it was made about 1 A.D., and for the Romans was a symbol of generation, while for the early Christians who had originally placed it in the forecourt of Old St. Peter's it symbolised the promise of eternal life, the fruit of the arbor vitae."

"The transformation of pagan symbols into Christian ones was one of the issues discussed by Thomas Hope in his Essay.

"The area of initiation and the creation of life leads . . . to the sanctuary is guarded . . .male and female figures, . . . they are turned inwards to look at each other across the altar on which are placed two large, open, candlesticks in alabaster carved in the form of the lotus flower, 'the emblem' as Lonsdale points out, 'of receptivity and reproduction' ".

Bullen concludes: "In a sense the whole chapel is a funerary monument, which does not so much memorialise death as celebrate the whole life process. Its inspiration was undoubtedly personal, triggered by the deaths in Sara's family and that of her sister in particular, but it is ultimately a monument to humankind caught up in the cycle of generation".

It is inevitable that St. Mary's Church attracts such various interpretations. It is a work that stands apart from any school, and there is little or no documentary or biographical guidance to its interpretation. It is such a complex and unusual work that it asks for the same response as a work of art or literature. It possesses that density and potential ambiguity of meaning that invites individual engagement and multiple readings. And, of course, it is interesting for people to respond to the richness of the work and bring their own thoughts and feelings to bear. The work is thereby enlarged.

However, the more interesting interpretation of the work will come from understanding the artist's intention and appreciating the circumstances, personal, social, cultural and historical, which produced the work.

Unfortunately, apart from the short memorandum which is concerned first and foremost with practical matters, we have nothing directly indicating Sarah Losh's intentions. Lonsdale says many things but, with his enthusiasm for cults and culture, he is an unreliable source who is likely to submerge any ideas he may have received from Sarah Losh in his own larger schemes. However, he does indicate that a wider reading than the strictly Anglican one espoused over-enthusiastically by Hall is probably right.

At present, we are only in a position to speculate on the origins of the work.

Some Speculative Concluding Remarks

We are able to glean some sense of Sarah Losh's character from the little we know of her life.

She was highly intelligent. Lonsdale's remarks comparing her to George Eliot and Madame de Stael may be making too great a claim, but she obviously impressed him and she impressed her Uncle James, who was a far more severe judge.

She was very well educated for a woman of her day. Her father had received the best of educations and, even though James was dismissive and suggested that his brother failed to make the most of his talents, he continued experimenting with things scientific and maintaining close intellectual contact with some of the leading scientific minds of his time. Similarly his personal and social connections suggest a man who was intellectually engaged in the wider political, social, literary and theological debates of his time. He was also keen on fossils and minerals. His contribution on mineralogy to Hutchinson's "The History of the County of Cumberland" is evidence of the depth of his interest. With William Paley as a close friend, he was intimate with one of the great minds of his generation. Paley is too readily impaled on the charge of "creationism" these days for us to truly appreciate how important an intellectual figure he was. His work on the justification of Christianity was at the leading edge of contemporary thought and, with its detailed considerations of the natural world, readily bridged our two cultures.

It is possible, although we have no evidence as such, that John Losh looked to his daughters as his heirs. His first son had died an infant and his second son, and nominally his heir, had severe mental limitations. It would not be surprising if Sarah did not receive the close attentions of a disappointed father. This might have been especially the case after the death of her mother.

William Gaskin, who was her tutor for a time, was an exceptionally able man. The anecdotes of his crossing intellectual swords with the erudite, forceful and argumentative Dean Milner, another great mind of his generation, testify to his intelligence and learning and he must have been a key influence on Sarah. He may also have set her an example of the retired intellectual life.

The tour on the continent was a formative experience in 1817. She was already thirty years old, and, I imagine, with her breadth of interests she had absorbed much that books and Britain had to offer, and that the continent, especially Italy, brought the depth of European culture alive for her. Certainly, the snippets we have from the travel journal - and Lonsdale rated it very highly - show an exceptional depth of informed engagement.

Her later reading, based on the slight evidence we have, shows that she continued to be keenly interested in the contemporary intellectual world. And her interests were very broad. Sarah may have read Scott, Lytton, Thackerey and Dickens, but she was also reading Harriet Martineau and Cobbett on matters social and political and was sufficiently absorbed by the theological tensions of the time to have a five volume set of Newman. Lonsdale's anecdote about her scorning Reichenbach suggests something of the enquiring breadth of her reading and we know that she read widely in science and history. She read deeply enough for Lonsdale to regard her as an authority on some subjects, such as the Corn Laws. This reading seems to have been the pursuit of a very able, cultivated woman, led by her own passionate curiosity rather than by any professional purpose or other ulterior motive.

She was, like her father and her uncles, involved in the intellectual life of the times, despite living in an out-of-the-way rural community. Carlisle, in the first half of the nineteenth century, perhaps because of its resident clerics and such politicians as Brougham and Howard, appears to have been a place for lively and informed debate. And Newcastle was a city, that, like Edinburgh, but on a smaller scale, had burgeoned during the enlightenment, and was buzzing with exciting ideas and enquiring minds. Industry, commerce and enterprise can be a stimulus to intellect and culture. The discoveries of fossils in the coal-mines and elsewhere prompted the work of Albany Hancock and others.

The opinions expressed on her Italian tour, especially in the Sistine Chapel and her view of Michelangelo, suggest a great clarity and independence of mind. She was no ready accepter of received opinions.

Sarah cultivated the arts. Lonsdale refers to poetry and other literary writings, though none have survived, and she painted and gardened on a grand and informed scale. It is possible that the paintings and the carving of the capitals in the apse are hers, and we know that she carved the alabaster font. Such work indicates a high level of artistic skill.

Sarah Losh's highly cultivated mind was marked by a rare independence and originality of judgment.

Her personal life was determined by her relationship with Katharine. We know next to nothing of Katharine and we only have glimpses of the two sisters together. They were rarely apart and they shared the same life. All enterprises, from the re-development of the house and estate to the erection of the memorial cross to their parents, were joint enterprises. The natural impression, and that given by Lonsdale, is that Sarah was the dominant partner, but this is not necessarily the case.

It might be surmised that their circumstances, particularly the loss of their mother when they were both around the age of puberty, caused Sarah and Katharine to be so close to each other. Neither married. But neither did many women in their family. Their father's only sister remained single and so did Sarah and Anne Bonner, their mother's sisters. Sarah Losh was an attractive and wealthy woman who moved in a wide social circle and, through family and social contacts, knew many people. Admittedly, she would not suffer fools gladly, but, although her intellect may have caused her to be seen as a blue-stocking, there is no reason to see why she did not, as most women did, get married. We, of course, know nothing of her sexuality, and it would be vain to speculate.

We do know that throughout her life, Sarah seems to have felt the death of close relatives very deeply. Her mother's death, when she was thirteen, and her father's death, fifteen years later, caused her a great deal of anguish, and she was bereft by Katharine's death in 1835, when she was almost fifty years old.

The return of George Losh and his family to the area and the other relatives who lived locally suggest that she maintained some sort of figure as head of the Losh family. And she continued to play the hostess at Woodside. There was an ascetic side to her nature. Lonsdale talks of her private study being in the bare attic rather than in the luxurious rooms below. However, in her will she displays a concern with many of the fine objects in her possession. In later life particularly, she acted the part of the benevolent country heiress, distributing money to local charities and taking a "paternal" interest in the community.

Of her personal manners as such we again know little. Lonsdale suggests she had her intimate friends, not least the formidable Jane Blamire. She was probably a stimulating conversationalist. She cared for animals. She could be severe. She certainly commanded a sharp pen and Lonsdale suggests that she taught herself to discipline her sharp tongue. And she was a formidable opponent. She wound the Vestry Committee round her little finger, but she also managed to get her own way, albeit over an out-of-the-way and insignificant rural church, with the Dean and the Chapter and the Bishop.

We are able to gather a little about her views on art. Writing about the Sistine Chapel, she said: "It is after all, but painting, and the more wonderful it is, the more it convinces one that the utmost faculties of man are inadequate to portray or even conceive of the things of future existence". She went further in suggesting that even Michelangelo in attempting to portray the things of the afterlife had lacked the intelligent sensibility and found himself overtaken by the empty, malicious and evil. She admires Correggio for suggesting paradise through his blissful figures who are only messengers and Guido Reni for his ability to suggest the ineffable through analogous sensations. We might infer that she is saying that it is impossible to describe the ultimate truths of religion through direct description. The only way is to indicate the nature of God and paradise through analogous representation. The created world of the church, the quiet beauty of its light, the delight in the breadth and detail of creation and the coherent rational symbolism of the whole may be such an analogous representation.

Sarah Losh was taken with the antique, such that she seems to draw spiritual sustenance from contemplating the works of the ancient world and the early church. Her use of Perranzabuloe and the Bewcastle Cross illustrates how she drew inspiration from a sense of the spirituality of the Early Church, but she never simply copied the earlier structures. She developed them and made them personal, significant and contemporary.

She did not adhere to any movement nor even appear to be drawn into the sensibility of the age. She was an eclectic in that she was willing to borrow anything that suited her purpose, but she was also possessed of a clear and strong vision such that she was able to make her borrowings her own.

We have no clear definition of Sarah Losh's religious views at a time when, perhaps more than many other times, people were examining their personal faith. However, Sarah's life gives some clues. Her comments on her travels, the ecumenical circle of her guests, and the breadth of her reading suggest that she did not adhere to a narrow or doctrinaire interpretation of Christianity and that she had an appreciation of pagan myth. She was committed to the Anglican Church. Her Uncle James was Unitarian, her friends, the Howards were Roman Catholic, for instance, and if she had been prompted to change faiths, there would have been little obstacle for such a determined and clear minded woman.

She built two churches. In Wreay she fought for total control and instituted several practices - the position of the altar, its stone structure and the candle-sticks - which were revolutionary in their implications. However, in Newton Arlosh she seems to have gone along with conventional practice and sought to do little that was different.

The Biblical texts she chose for the Cross and her gravestone ("The Lord is my light and my salvation"; "Be merciful unto me, O God, be merciful unto me; for my soul trusteth in Thee: and under the shadow of Thy wings shall be my refuge" and, "Lord let thy mercy lighten upon us") indicate a strong belief in a personal god who is merciful and offers salvation in an after-life. Sarah Losh's own words on the Cross ("May this sign of consolation cast its shadow on the grave of John Losh and his wife Isabella. Souls well beloved, may you walk safe through the midst of the shadow of death. Farewell till the times of refreshing from the presence of the Lord.") speak of the cross as a sign of consolation, that is of the possibility of an after-life through Christ's death on the cross and of a time when the souls of the dead shall be in "the presence of the Lord". There can be no clearer statement of the central tenets of Christian belief. The other personal statement ("Two daughters purposed that this stone should be set up; one performed it, greatly sorrowing".) suggests that it was not an easily held belief, but one adopted alongside a deeply felt sense of the tragedy of life.

The Church of St. Mary best illustrates her religious views and should be read as such. At the heart of the church is the chancel. The carefully orchestrated light creates a spiritual stillness about the altar. The image of the altar is one where the wheat and the grapes - the bread and the wine - are at the base, and rising through the wings of the renaissance eagles, they support the elaborate communion table and become the substance of the communion.

The eye is led to the image of the lamb of God, the image of Christ as proclaimed by John the Baptist, "who taketh away the sins of the world". This is re-inforced by the increasing intensity towards the centre of the seven lights, illuminated by natural light, in the wall above. Around the wall, to either side of the lamb, are the apostles with the words of the Apostles Creed, one of the earliest statements of the faith of the Early Church: "I believe in God the Father Almighty, Maker of heaven and earth: And in Jesus Christ his only Son our Lord, Who was conceived by the Holy Ghost, Born of the Virgin Mary, Suffered under Pontius Pilate, Was crucified, dead, and buried, He descended into hell; The third day he rose again from the dead, He ascended into heaven, And sitteth on the right hand of God the Father Almighty; From thence he shall come to judge the quick and the dead. I believe in the Holy Ghost; The holy Catholic Church; The Communion of Saints; The Forgiveness of Sins; The Resurrection of the body, And the life everlasting". Sarah Losh could not have chosen to put a more solid declaration of the Christian faith at the heart of the church. However, the clarity of this statement appears strangely compromised by the naive, even playful, emblems of the apostles. It may be that her intention is to get away from the conventional response to the worthy representations of the saints and to look at them and the words afresh. Throughout her work there seems to be an attempt to return to the simplicity and directness of the early faith.

The wall above is decorated with flowers, perhaps roses, lilies and passion flowers, each of which has a traditional symbolic connotation. However, the wall of painted flowers surrounds the deep window embrasures, the central ones of which carry designs based on fossils. The relationship between the fossil world and the natural world is one that is repeated elsewhere in the church. The capitals above the sedilia carry plant forms that in some cases might also be fossil forms.

The underlying idea displayed by the chancel may well be the Christian communion at the heart of universal design that relates the creed and the natural and fossil worlds. It is not an idea too far removed from Paley's argument for the existence of God from design. The deviant elements of the bat, and the bird and the lizard and the serpent lurk at the edges, on the extreme pillars, and may threaten or be incorporated in the design.

Beyond the chancel, the cultured heads, seem to represent man and woman contemplating the design. The angels and archangels seem less divine creatures and more human in their individuality and their bearing. It is as though before the design of the universe, they are given wings. The bat and the dragon are not so much trodden underfoot, but the winged figures rise above them. The pulpit carved from the bog oak in the form of a fossil presents the message of God coming out of the design of the natural world and the stork and eagle bear the word of God upwards on their wings. This may be a created world that is analogous to paradise.

The clerestory windows consist of a fossil design between two flowers; the windows below, create a harmonious whole from the fragments of the past. The windows in the west end offer a more intense harmony, the glass is richer and the pattern more compressed and at the centre of two of the windows is the image of the cross.

Outside, the images around the windows on the west end, so precise in their delineation, show design in the variety of life, from the fossil world, on the earth and in the air. The "gargoyles" around the church may simply be the variety of creation, but they may also be derived from fossil forms and, in their ambiguity, demonstrate how the forms found in the fossils are represented in the natural world.

The cones are a central image. They mark the entrance to the nave and the ones that hang from the roof measure its length. A cone is both part of the natural world and has the qualities of a fossil. It appears to be dead and yet it is the bearer of life, a living symbol of rebirth and resurrection.

The motifs of the water-lily, lotus flower, the gourd and others used throughout the church are, obviously, images of natural life, but they are images that carry a wide range of cultural significances belonging to Christian and non-Christian mythologies. Without any indication from Sarah Losh as to what they meant to her, we can read them in diverse ways, ranging from the pagan to the ecclesiological. Many commentators have noted the absence of the cross and other Christian imagery. This is not unusual for a church of this date. The cross was felt to be Catholic imagery and, if present, would not have been placed at the centre of the church. There is, in fact, a conspicuous amount of Christian imagery for an Anglican church of the time: the wheat and grapes on the communion table, the Apostles Creed and the images of the apostles and the "Ecce Agnus Dei" and the crosses found in the windows and other associated images elsewhere.

The arrow in the wall is the one discordant element. It can only refer to the death of William Thain and, since Sarah Losh must have heard of his death in terrifying circumstances when the church was being built, it represents, in its brutality, an outburst of despair. An outburst that goes directly against her strong determination that a church should celebrate life and not death.

There is throughout the work of Sarah Losh a recurrent theme of rebirth, renewal, resurrection. The bog oak is resurrected. The fragments of stained glass are brought back to life. The old wood of the pews becomes part of the roof. The old chapel becomes the new. The oil lamps from Pompeii, the imitated Norman apse, the pine cones and the fossils, the Apostles Creed and the liturgical forms of the early church are renewed.

Within all things, the natural world and the fossil record, the worlds of religion and culture she finds the possibility of rebirth and renewal. It is as though it is a pattern inherent in the design of nature itself.

As Sarah Losh stated so adamantly, the church is not a place for images of death. The Church of St. Mary at Wreay celebrates the glory and diversity of life and shows how the Christian God is at the heart of the design.

Such a reading as the above is speculative, but it has the virtue of being based on the little we know of Sarah Losh's life and opinions. It is only when we know more about her life and recover more of her views that we can arrive at a more secure interpretation. Such an interpretation must take fully into account the rich individual detail of so much of the work and determine exactly what it might signify as part of the overall design. Such a complex design will not, and should not, yield up its meaning too readily.

For the time being we are left with a profound, truly original, and beautiful work of art.

APPENDICES

Appendix A) Sarah Losh's Will

Below is a copy of the codicil Sarah Losh made to her first will and a copy of her second will.

Codicil to first will

"I Sarah Losh of Woodside spinster make, this codicil of my will commencing with the following list of articles or small items in lieu of cash which I leave as remembrances to relatives and friends-

Mr Liddell £10 or a book or inkstand

Mr Losh Possible Pleasant moyen age monumental

Mr Gale £10

Mr Townley £10 - heads by Dapper from Michaelangelo & Raphael

Mr Postlethwaite £10 an oil sketch of Tynemouth, now in south entrance

Mr R Losh £10

Miss Townley £5

Mr Bonner - collection - silver pot with silver teapot which was Mrs J Bonners (crossed out)

Mr J Warwick £10 curio oleoate

Mrs C Warwick £10

Miss Kemmis and Miss Cussans each one of my Roman mosaics to be set for a broach

Mr W. S. Losh Japan dessert set given by Wm M Losh - & inlaid chest of drawers in outer passage

Mr W. S. Losh Billings Carlisle Cathedral

Mr James Losh junior - medal cabinet now in {taissance}

Miss Alicia M. Losh - Montfaucon

Mr Hutchinson £10 & cedar wardrobe

Miss Hutchinson £5 & Parlour l'antiquite enpleque -

Miss E Hutchinson £5

Mr Williamson £5

Miss Anna Hutchinson £5

Mrs Player £10

Miss Elenor Anderson £5

Mrs Mayhew £10

Miss Boyd £5

Miss Catherine Mayhew £10

Mr Ramsay £10 & large inkstand made at Birmingham after that of Petrarch

Miss Graham £5

Mr Graham £5. Mrs Rankin- Glossary of architecture given me by Mr Stamper to be rebound

Miss Blamire £5

Miss Oates Williams's Greece

Mr Jackson B_____

Mr A Donald mahogony chest of drawers in back room & Cooks geography

Mr J Scott the bureau chest of drawers in back room

Miss Shepherd the other mahogany chest of drawers in back room (and my clothes.) [added in different hand]

Mary - my bedding & washing stand

Miss Agnes Lowe the broach left me by Mr Cooper.

Mr Moffat B_____'s History of Matter

My Verona inkstand to be chained in Wreay Chapel

Of all personal effects not included in the above list I dispose of as follows; I leave to my cousin John Warwick the following articles of plate - viz. 1 silver kettle & lamp 1 tankard - 4 bottle slides 2 small open baskets - 1 bead basket 1 small tea pot 1 fish slice/ladle 1 set of cruets & 1 small waiters all my other articles of silver or plated goods or hardware of any sort glass china crockery linen wine or household stores of any description I leave to my cousin Alicia M. Losh ---- to my cousin James Losh the paintings books & furniture -- breakfast room & dining room/except those otherwise named/ also the large painting in the old staircase & large landscape in the study & the portrait of the writer Holcraft - also articles in the north and south entrances but not in the intermediate ones - also the furniture of the best north bed room & dressing room & the two balcony rooms & dressing rooms and the 2 rooms over the kitchen & all the servants bedrooms kitchen store parlour servants hall laundry workhouse stables barn & coach house - also all out of doors stock on the premises - all other things whether furniture pictures prints books & miscellaneous articles in all other rooms passages chests & closets with all articles writings drawings of my own I leave to my cousin Alicia M Losh. - I except only the oak desk in the bathroom & the iron chest both which which contain papers & memoranda belonging to the estate & these must go along with it - and I constitute my cousin James both my principal heir & residuary estate.

Copied sealed & delivered this twenty third day of December A.D. 1851 in the presence of us who have in the presence of each other thereunto set our hands & seals

sig. Sarah Losh

Mary Bowes

Mary Ann Richardson

Having made a new will signed this day, but not having found it needful to alter the codicil to the former will, I now confirm it & sign it now, in presence of the following persons, who will append their signatures after me - signed sealed & delivered this fourth day of September A.D. 1852 in the presence of us who have in the presence of each other thereunto set our hands & seals

Sarah Losh

Mary Bowes

Mary Ann Richardson

Sarah Losh's Second Will made in 1852

Richard Jackson Commissioner

I Sarah Losh of Woodside spinster make this my last will & testament & appoint as executors of the same my cousins James Losh & his brother W.S. Losh & William S. Moffat of Briscoe - I leave to the said W. S. Losh & his wife Sarah Losh their heirs and assigns forever all the lands & buildings purchased at Wreay by my late sister & me from the Robinson family as shown in the plan part of which land my said cousin is already the owner of - I leave to my cousin Margaret Alicia Losh the whole land purchased at Ravenside by my late sister & me of the late Mr Langrigg with all buildings new & old thereon, also the stripes of plantations on the south side thereof & the large field lying in front of the house at Ravenside adjoining the Ravensbrook - to her her heirs & assigns for ever - I leave to the trustees of my cousin Frances Hutchinson the cottage at Briscoe, the new inhabits & the garden wherein it stands for her her heirs & assigns for ever - I leave all the rest of my landed property (with all buildings thereto appertaining) of whatever denomination & wherever situated subject to my past debts & personal expenses & to all annuities hereinafter to be enumerated & moreover to any legacies hereinafter to be enumerated in this paper or in a codicil should they exceed the funds available for this object at my death. I leave the landed property & buildings thus charged & liable to my cousin James Losh for his life & after to his lawful male issue failing whom to my cousin John Losh after to his lawful male issue failing whom to my cousin Robert H. Losh to his lawful male issue failing whom to my cousin William Septimus Losh & his lawful male issue - failing such to the lawful female issue of my cousins James, John, Robert H and William Septimus Losh successively - failing all such to my cousin Cecilia Gale & her issue male or female - failing which to my cousin Margaret Townley & her issue male or female - failing which to my cousin Jemima Postlethwaite & her issue male or female - successively all in like manner successively to the issues male or female failing all these in like manner successively to the daughters of my uncle George Losh & the daughters of my uncle William Losh their heirs & assigns forever. the property so contractcd I charge with the following life annuities - I leave my cousin Alicia M. Losh one hundred pounds a year for her life & to the trustees of my cousin Frances Hutchinson fifty pounds a year for her life & that of her husband & I leave fifty pounds a year to the trustees of my cousin Georgina Cussans for her life - payments to be half-yearly - and whereas my late aunt Margaret Losh left to Frances Hutchinson & Alicia M Losh the annuities of £50 & £30, which bequests were not properly enactuated & are encumbered (altho they have always been paid) I feel as her executor I ought to rectify, I secure the said bequests on my own entailed property namely of fifty pounds a year to Frances Hutchinson for her life & that of her husband & thirty pounds a year to Alicia M. Losh for her life - I leave ten pounds a year for her life to Hannah Shepherd & five pounds per year for their lives to Robert Donald, George Davidson & John Armstrong of my property in money wherever vested or owing to me I dispose as follows I leave to my cousin Alicia M. Losh three thousand pounds - I leave to the trustees of my cousin Frances Hutchinson two thousand pounds the interest to be paid to her during her life & afterwards the principal to be shared by her daughters in equal portions I leave two thousand five hundred pounds to be applied towards reducing the debt to the property at Birtley of which my cousin John Warwick is the proprietor but in which his mother & sister have a life's interest & if at my death anything be due from them to me I leave the same to his mother Frances Warwick such such balance occur I leave to the trustees of Anna Rankin four hundred pounds & to the children of the late William Gaskin one hundred pounds - I leave two hundred pounds to my cousin Mary Kemmis one hundred pounds to my cousin Sarah Losh & one hundred pounds to my cousin Georgina Cussans - one hundred pounds to my cousin W. S. Losh & one hundred pounds to William S. Moffatt. I leave fifteen pounds to Hetherington Smallwood - five pounds cash to his mother & sister I leave to Mary Packer & her sister Catherine & to Isabella Robson five pounds each - to William Bull & Joseph Scott ten pounds each & mourning to the servants at Woodside & to George Davidson & John Armstrong - Also mourning to Sarah Armstrong & Mary Donald & Esther Sheard - ten pounds to Mr Jackson & five to the Wreay poor at my funeral which must be as private & inexpensive as possible - I leave to the blind orphans at Newcastle the school at Upperby & dispensary at Carlisle £20 each - all these sums & bequests & all others in my codicil I charge on my entailed landed property should the money belonging to me or due to me at my death not suffice - for their liquidation therefore I charge them on my property and as well personal excepting only that part of the land left to my cousins Alicia M. Losh - W. S. Losh Frances Hutchinson - I appoint my cousin James Losh . . . . legatee - of him I desire the old poney may be taken care

201

of as at present & the old carriage horse also
    signed sealed & delivered
    this fourth day
    of September A.D. 1851
    in the presence of us who
    in presence of each other
    have herewith set our
    hands & seals

Sarah Losh
Mary Bowes
Mary Ann Richardson

Note: The will was actually written in 1852 and the witnesses were required to take an oath to assert the correct date.

Appendix B) A List of Sara Losh's Works

This list of works is derived from the one compiled by Katharine Drew.

1) Woodside South Front Restoration, (post 1786, pre 1826) *The original house has 14th century foundations. Sarah, with Katharine, restored and redesigned the South front, enlarged and modernised the rest of the house, and laid out the garden. The house passed from Sarah to James Losh, then to James Arlosh. In 1904 he left it to Manchester Unitarian College, Oxford, who sold it almost immediately. In 1936 it was partially demolished.*

2) Dame's Infants' School (c .1828) *Now Wreay Syke Fold, with several later additions.*

3) Schoolhouse. (1830) *The school replaced an earlier one of 1760, before which time the Chapel was used. An infant room was built out on a wing to the north when the Dame's school closed. In 1874 W. S. Losh added a village library. From 1906 to 1910 further improvements were carried out, extending the main room, re-roofing and erecting new outbuildings. Sarah's school survives from the east wall, dated 1830, as far as the new door and porch.*

4) Pompeian Cottage (1830) *Built as a schoolmaster's cottage, a replica of a house excavated at Pompeii, which Sarah had visited in 1817.*

5) Oratory or Isolation Chapel (c.1835-1840) *A copy of St Perran-in-the-Sands uncovered by the sands in 1835. Single storey, 29 foot x 16' foot, 13 foot high. Chapel consecrated 12 May, 1842.*

6) Sexton's Cottage (c.1835-1840) *Dated 1835 by DoE, probably slightly later, but before 1840*

7) Cemetery (c.1835-1840) *Walled acre of land with gates. Consecrated 12 May, 1842.*

8) Losh Burial Enclosure (1840-42)

9) Sundial (1840-42)

10) Bewcastle Cross (1840-42) *Copied from original late 7th century Cross at Bewcastle, Cumbria.*

11) St. Mary's Church, Wreay (1840-42)

12) Newton Arlosh Church Restoration (1843) *Much of Sarah Losh's work in the church interior was changed when the altar was changed and placed on the north end in 1895.*

15) Wreay Syke *(pre 1847) Built by William Septimus Losh, but signs of Sarah's influence.*

14) Mausoleum (c.1847) *DoE dating 1850, but the building is in "Mannix and Whellan's Directory" of 1847; statue of Katharine by Dunbar is dated "1850".*

16) Bell Well (date not known, but post 1840) *Built using the bell gable of the old Chapel.*

17) Katharine's Well (*Dated 1867 but this refers to a restoration. Lonsdale says it was built by Sarah)*

18) St. Ninian's Well, Brisco (*date not known, but probably 1830s)*

19 Design for Wetheral Bridge (?1829) *Mentioned by Lonsdale.*

Appendix C) The Losh Family

John, 'the Big Black Squire', of Woodside, (Sarah's grandfather) born circa 1723. Buried at St. Cuthbert's, Carlisle on 13 April, 1789. Married (1 November, 1755, at St. Cuthbert's) **Catherine**, baptised 25 September, 1729, at Burgh-by-Sands, daughter of John Liddell of Moorhouse, Burgh-by-Sands. She was buried at St. Cuthbert's, on 9 April, 1789.

Children of John and Catherine Losh: *(Sarah's father uncles and aunt. Their children, i.e. Sarah Losh's generation, are indented.)*

John, partner in the Walker Alkali Works, Newcastle-upon-Tyne, High Sheriff of Cumberland in 1811, Provincial Grand Master for Cumberland, baptised 29 March, 1757, at St. Cuthbert's, Carlisle, educated Sedburgh & Trinity Hall, Cambridge, admitted to the Middle Temple on 1 April, 1775. He died 31 March 1814, buried at Wreay. Married 20 December, 1784, at Boldon, **Isabella**, daughter of Thomas Bonner of Callerton Hall, near Newcastle. She died 7 October, 1799, aged 33, buried at Wreay.

> **Children of John and Isabella Losh** *(Sarah and her siblings.)*
>
> **Sarah,** born 1 January, 1786, at Woodside, baptised 6 January, 1786, at St. Cuthbert's, Carlisle, died unmarried 29 March, 1853, at Woodside. Buried at Wreay.
>
> **John**, Buried at St. Cuthbert's, Carlisle, aged 5 weeks, on 17 January, 1787. His name is on his parents' grave in Wreay.
>
> **Katharine Isabella**, baptised 11 February, 1788, at St. Cuthbert's, Carlisle, died unmarried and was buried at Wreay on 26 February, 1835.
>
> **Joseph**, b. circa 1789, died 17 January, 1848, and was buried at Wreay, aged 59, on 21 January, 1848.

William, baptised 23 August, 1758, at St. Cuthbert's, Carlisle. Died after a fall from a tree and was buried at St. Cuthbert's on 5 April, 1768.

Joseph, Lieutenant, 7th Dragoon Guards, baptised 30 May, 1760, at St. Cuthbert's, Carlisle, died 16 July, 1784. Buried at St. Mary de Crypt, Gloucester.

James, M.A., of Jesmond Grove, Newcastle-upon-Tyne. Born 10 June, 1763, at Woodside, baptised 12 June, 1763, at St. Cuthbert's, Carlisle. Educated Penrith, Sedburgh & Trinity College, Cambridge. Admitted to Lincoln's Inn on 16 November, 1789. Recorder of Newcastle, 1832-33. He died 23 September, 1833, at Greta Bridge and was buried at Gosforth on 3 October, 1833. He married. 1 February, 1798, at Aldingham, Lancashire, **Cecilia**, daughter of Rev Roger Baldwin, D.D., Rector of Aldingham, near Ulverston, Lancashire. She lived later at the Grange, Cartmel and died in 1842.

> **Children of James and Cecilia Losh:** *(Sarah's cousins)*
>
> **James Henry,** baptised 17 December, 1799, at St. Andrew's, Newcastle. Died 25 February, 1800. Buried at St. Nicholas, Gosforth on 27 February, 1800.
>
> **William Liddell**, baptised 15 September, 1802, at St. Andrew's, Newcastle. Died 4 May, 1803. Buried at St. Nicholas, Gosforth on 6 May, 1803.
>
> **James,** M.A., of Woodside, baptised 21 September, 1803, at St. Andrew's, Newcastle. Educated Durham Grammar School & Trinity College, Cambridge. Admitted to Lincoln's Inn on 6 November, 1824. Judge of the County Courts in Northumberland 1853-58, Chairman of the Newcastle and Carlisle Railway, Alderman of Newcastle. Died 1 October, 1858, at 28 Clayton Street West, Newcastle.

Baldwin, baptised 7 April, 1805, at St. Andrew's, Newcastle, married 31 July, 1856, at Old Church, St. Pancras, **Gertrude Jane Harding**. Later of Jesmond Lodge, Winton, Ryde, Isle of Wight, Lieutenant, 23rd Fusiliers. Retired from the Army in 1833. He died 18 Feb 1887 at Ryde. She died. 17 October, 1908, at Jesmond, Ryde.

John Joseph. Born 30 March, 1806, baptised 20 August, 1806, at St. Andrew's, Newcastle. Educated Durham Grammar School & Queen's College, Cambridge. Lieutenant Colonel, 42nd Madras Native Infantry, Military Auditor of Madras. Served Ava 1824-26, Coorg 1834. Died 12 March, 1862, at Wreay Syke and was buried at Wreay.

Robert Henry Baptised 8 September, 1808, at St. Andrew's, Newcastle. Died 7 November, 1867, at Langarth Cottage, Brisco. Buried at Wreay.

William Septimus. Baptised 16 March, 1810, at St. Andrew's, Newcastle. Married 21 May, 1831, at the British Embassy Chapel, Paris, his first cousin, Sarah Spencer, daughter of George Losh. She died 1883 and he died 24 September, 1888, at Woodside. They were both buried at Wreay.

Cecilia Isabella. Baptised 30 September, 1801, at St. Andrew's, Newcastle. Married 29 July, 1820, at St. Andrew's, her first cousin, William Gale, J.P., of Bardsea Hall, Ulverston, son of Lieutenant General Henry Richmond Gale and his wife Sarah, daughter of Rev Roger Baldwin, D.D. He died 30 November, 1865, and she died 29 September, 1866.

Margaret Catherine. Born 12 April, 1813, at Jesmond, married 1836 at Cartmel, Lancashire, Edmund Townley.

Thomas (twin), Baptised 24 February, 1766, at St. Cuthbert's, Carlisle. Buried at Hesket-in-the-Forest on 11 March, 1766.

George (twin), of Saltwellside, Gateshead, County Durham, merchant and manufacturer, with iron works at Balgonie, Fife and Rouen, lived in France for a long period, baptised 24 February 1766 at St. Cuthbert's, Carlisle, married 28 November 1796 at St. Cuthbert's, Carlisle, **Frances,** daughter of Joseph Wilkinson of Carlisle. She was buried in Paris on 26 Jan 1828 and he died 3 April 1846 at Low Heaton having had issue:

Children of George and Frances Losh: *(Sarah's cousins)*

Mary Alice. Baptised 18 March, 1798, at Gateshead. Married 13 December, 1817, at the British Embassy Chapel, Paris, **James Kemmis,** M.A., of Derry with Meelick, Queen's Co., Ireland and Choisy, near Paris. He died July, 1840, and she died 31 December, 1875. Buried at Wreay having had issue.

Frances Elizabeth. Baptised 26 April, 1799, at Gateshead. Married 29 July, 1820, at St. Andrew's, Newcastle, **Francis Coleridge Hutchinson**, M.D., of Douglas, Isle of Man. He died 6 October, 1863, at Brisco. She died 22 November, 1878, at The Cottage, Brisco. They were both buried at Wreay having had issue: 3 sons and 8 daughters.

Margaret Alicia. Later of Ravenside, near Carlisle. Died unmarried 20 March, 1872, at Abbotsleigh, Upper Norwood.

Sarah Spencer. Born circa 1809, m. 21 May, 1831, at the British Embassy Chapel, Paris, her first cousin, **William Septimus Losh** and had issue (see above).

Georgina Cecilia Thomasina. Married 2 July, 1834, at the British Embassy Chapel, Paris, Major **Thomas Cussans**, 94th Foot, son of James Cussans of Amity Hall, and his wife Catherine. He died 22 August, 1855, at Le Havre and she died 1857.

Robert (twin), baptised 16 February, 1768, at St. Cuthbert's, Carlisle. Died unmarried, 27 October, 1787, in Pilgrim Street, Newcastle-upon-Tyne.

William. Baptised 26 June, 1771, at St. Cuthbert's, Carlisle. Educated Hamburg, married 1 March, 1798, at Gateshead, **Alice,** daughter of Joseph Wilkinson of Carlisle. Later of Point Pleasant, Northumberland, manager of Walker Alkali Works, Newcastle, Consul for Sweden and Prussia in Newcastle. She died 31 January, 1859, at Ellison Place, Newcastle. He died 4 August, 1861, at Ellison Place, Newcastle having had issue:

> **Children of William and Alice Losh:** *(Sarah's cousins)*
>
> **John.** Died 16 April, 1800, aged 9 months, and was buried at St. Nicholas, Gosforth, on 18 April, 1800.
>
> **Alice.** Baptised 12 October, 1802, at St. Andrew's, Newcastle, married 1 August, 1822, at St. Peter's, Wallsend, **James Crosby Anderson**. He died 1837 having had issue and she then married Mr. Player and died circa 1858 having had further issue.
>
> **Margaret**. Born 30 July, 1803, baptised 28 July, 1818, at St. Peter's, Wallsend, married 2 March, 1822, at St. Peter's, Wallsend, her first cousin, **Spencer,** thirteenth laird of Penkill Castle, Girvan, Ayrshire, elder son of Spencer Boyd of Penkill and his wife Sarah, daughter of Joseph Wilkinson of Carlisle.

Margaret (twin). Baptised 16 February, 1768, at St. Cuthbert's, Carlisle. Died unmarried 29 December, 1845, and was buried at Wreay on 1 January, 1846.

Appendix D) Select Bibliography

This bibliography lists only those works which refer to Sarah Losh and the Church.

Bell Scott, W.: *Autobiographical Notes,* ed. W. Minto, London. 1892.

Bullen, J.B.: *Continental Crosscurrents: British Criticism and European Art, 1810-1910.*

Bullen, J.B.: *Sara Losh: architect, romantic, mythologist:* THE BURLINGTON MAGAZINE; Number 1184; Volume CXLIII; November 2001.

Drew, Katherine: *Dissertation for B. Arch.* for Newcastle University, 1985. (Copy in Carlisle Library)

Hall, The Rev. A. R.: *Wreay.* Chas. Thurnam and Sons, Carlisle,1929.

Hall, Marshall: *The Artists of Cumbria: An Illustrated Dictionary of Cumberland, Westmorland, North Lancashire and North West Yorkshire Painters, Sculptors, Draughtsmen and Engravers Born Between 1615 and 1900. Marshall Hall Associates, Kendal, 1979.*

Hill, Rosemary: *Romantic Affinities, Crafts, no.166 [2000],* pp.35-39.

Jenkins, Simon: *England's Thousand Best Churches.* Allen Lane 1999.

Kemp, Laurie: *Woodside.* Wreay, 1997.

Lonsdale, Dr. Henry: *The Worthies of Cumberland. Volume Four.* George Routledge. 1873

Losh, James: The manuscript *Diaries 1798-1833,* are kept in Carlisle Library.

Losh, James: *The Diaries and Correspondence of James Losh,* ed. E. HUGHES, Surtees Society, 1963.

Mannix and Whellan: *History, Gazetteer and Directory of Cumberland, 1847.* Beverley. 1847

Mee, Arthur: *The King's England: The Lake Counties: Cumberland and Westmorland.* Hodder and Stoughton. 1937.

Nicholson, Norman: *Greater Lakeland.* Robert Hale, 1969

Pevsner, Nikolaus: *The Buildings of England: Cumberland and Westmorland.* Penguin. 1967.

Pevsner, Nikolaus: 'Sara Losh's Church', Architectural Review, CXLII. 1967.

Plouviez: *Sara Losh. The Oxford Dictionary of National Biography.* Oxford. 2004.

Robinson, John Martin: *The Architecture of Northern England.* MacMillan, 1986.

Rossetti: *Letters of Dante Gabriel Rossetti,* ed. O. Doughty and J. R. Wahl. 1967.

Stevenson, Jane: *A Woman's Touch in Stone, The Guardian,,* Saturday ,August 20, 2005

Topping, George: *Rambles in the Borderland with the "Clan".* Charles Thurnam, Carlisle. 1921

Wreay Church and Evolution is an uncredited article in *Geology Today Volume 21 Issue 1,* Page 2 - January 2005

The Cumbria Record Office in Carlisle contains the Jackson Notebook, the *Minute Book of the Minister and Trustees of Wreay Chapel* and other documents. PR 118.

Carlisle Library has the manuscript volumes of James Losh's Diaries and Katherine Drew's Dissertation.